Yes, You Can...

Afford to Raise a Family

Yes, You Can...
Afford to Raise a Family

CREATED BY SAM GOLLER

WITH

JAMES E. STOWERS

JACK JONATHAN

DR. SHEELAGH MANHEIM

DEBORAH SHOUSE

ALEXIS PRESTON

ILLUSTRATED BY

PAUL COKER, JR.

Discover the good life!™

STOWERS INNOVATIONS
INC

An American Century Company

Yes, You Can… Afford to Raise a Family
First Edition
©2004 by Stowers Innovations, Inc.
All rights reserved. Printed in the United States of America. First printing.

For information write:
Stowers Innovations, Inc.
4500 Main Street, Kansas City, Missouri 64111-7709.

ISBN 0-9629788-5-X: $19.95
Library of Congress Control Number: 2003112464

When we were first married, my wife, Virginia, and I both worked. However, long before our first child was born, we decided that when we had kids one of us would adapt our employment status to part-time. Virginia was better at managing the demands of the household, and my earning potential was greater than hers, so we agreed that I would continue to work full-time and she would cut back her work to four or five hours a day in order to have more time with the kids.

This was an easy decision for us to make. It supported one of the fundamental values we wanted to keep in raising our family. More challenging though, was preparing to live on a reduced income.

Because we were worried about becoming dependent on a two-income lifestyle, we decided to live only on my earnings, while saving and investing all of Virginia's salary. This decision proved to be the right one for us. This strategy prevented us the shock of being forced to drastically reduce our standard of living when our children were born.

More importantly, it gave us a solid financial foundation on which we could build our future success.

With the information in this book, you can create a stable financial home life while living your parenting dreams.

James E. Stowers

Founder and Chairman of the Board, American Century Companies
Co-Founder, Stowers Institute for Medical Research
Author of *Yes, You Can ... Achieve Financial Independence*

The creation of a book such as this is rarely the result of a single person's effort. Therefore, it is fitting that those who helped be recognized for their contributions.

Jim Stowers deserves the first tip of the hat. It's because of his dedication to helping people improve their financial position that this book even exists.

A special thanks goes to Jack Jonathan, creator of *Yes, You Can ... Raise Financially Aware Kids*. The experience of working with him on that book provided the stimulus for this book.

Alexis Preston had the difficult role of editor – meticulously reading each word (again and again) to make certain they were assembled in a way that made sense. She also coordinated and incorporated the changes presented to us by our editorial board.

Deborah Shouse took the first step in getting this book off the ground. Her talent in organization and writing provided the basis for this book to evolve to what it is today.

Paul Coker, Jr. and Frank Addington took the words on paper and made them come to life. Through Paul's illustrations and Frank's design, this book is truly "fun and easy-to-read."

Dr. Sheelagh Manheim contributed her expertise in the area of child psychology to make certain the ideas presented in this book are in the best interest of the children.

Special appreciation to Pam Hayes-Bohanan, Sara Burke, Tiffany Crabtree, Darlene Fairchild, Kelly Finn, Lisa Waterman Gray, Gwen Jones, Judy Korb, Lucy Lauer, Virginia Lore, Sharon Louk, Susan Schlinsog, Diana and Lee Stuart, Jodi Trana and Stephen Tucker for their willingness to share their money stories and the lessons they've learned.

Thanks also to Lisa Waterman Gray, Mike Higgins, Mary-Lane Kamberg, Linda Kincaid, Neil Neumeyer, Nancy O'Neill, Candy Schock, Barb Throm, Lee Vogel and Virginia Bruce-Wolfe, Ph.D. who all served on our editorial board.

The final nod is to you, the reader. Thank you for caring enough about your family and financial future to take the time to learn the essential facts about money.

Sam Goller

Sam Goller

Co-Author of *Yes, You Can ... Raise Financially Aware Kids*
Creator National Cut-Up-Your-Credit-Card Day™ - October 16

Part One - Family and Money Matters

Chapter 1

Putting a Price Tag on the Priceless – The High Cost of Childhood

There is a stark reality when it comes to raising a child … it isn't cheap. And while many parents will try to do it with minimal financial planning, the experience can be more rewarding with a well thought-out strategy.

- **Perfection Unlimited**
- **The Financial Facts of Life**
- **On Your Mark, Get Set, Go!**
- **From Pre-School to Behind the Wheel**
- **Did You Say College?**
- **So, Now What?**

Is money everything?

Chapter 2 35

Taking the First Step – Determine Your Priorities

Most of us can list what we think makes a good parent. This list represents the principles and values we cannot afford to compromise.

- **What Values are Most Important to You in Raising Your Family?**
- **What Does Money Mean to You?**
- **Money Talks**
- **Understanding Your Priorities**
- **Where are You Now?**

Chapter 3 51

Where Does Your Money Go?

In order to fully understand how money fits into your family life, you need to take a close look at how you are spending your money.

- **Tracking the Wandering Dollar**
- **Getting Organized: The Ultimate Money Order**
- **Taming the Wild Expenses: Developing a Budget**
- **Closing the Gap Between Income and Expenses**
- **Time, Money and DETERMINATION**

Chapter 4 73

The Price of Employment

For some people, the income they earn is just enough to pay for the cost of working. If you're in a two-income family, can you live on one income? If you are a one-income family, what strategies can you use to stretch your money further?

- **Values vs. Income – The Big Balancing Act**
- **What's My Salary Really Worth?**
- **Income Reduction – Living on Less**
- **One Plus: Bridging the Earnings Gap**

Chapter 5 93

You Are What You Buy

How you spend your money is a reflection of your family's values. Take some time to understand your spending decisions.

- **Matching Your Values with Your Spending**
- **Home Works**
- **Driving a Good Bargain**
- **Make the Most of Windfalls, Raises and Other Extras**
- **Saving Without Suffering: Tips for Reducing Expenses**

Tracking the wandering dollar.

The attack of the unexpected.

Educate Yourself On College Plans and Savings

Take a quick course on the many ways you can save and pay for your child's education.

Life Insurance

Here's everything you need to know about life insurance in "terms" you can easily understand.

Spending Time Without Spending Lots of Money

More than 70 fun ideas help you enjoy playing, exploring and learning with your family on a limited budget.

Getting Your Family Off to the Right Start

One of the key factors to financial freedom is defining your family's values, including the role money plays in your life. That's why, throughout this book, you will be invited to define your priorities and understand how you think about money.

Whether you're a rookie parent-to-be or a veteran with a house full of kids, the information in this book will help you make smart decisions as you travel down the uncertain path of parenthood. Even if your nest is empty, you will discover new ways to think about money, look at life and share your experiences with your grown kids.

To help you on your parenting journey, this book is divided into two parts:

Part One - Family and Money Matters

Family and Money Matters provides you the opportunity to look in-depth at what money means to you and includes practical information about the different ways money can impact your life.

Part Two - A Closer Look

A Closer Look is filled with specific details and answers to some of parents' most frequently asked questions.

Throughout this book, you will read stories from other parents. These are included so you can see that you are not alone in the challenges you are facing. Hopefully, you will learn from their mistakes and find inspiration in their successes.

As you read through the following pages, you will be asked to answer many questions. Regardless of how you answer, you should always consider one more question … are the decisions you make good for your family?

By focusing your efforts on what's best for your family and your children, you can begin to realize both the joys of financial freedom and the priceless experience of having kids. This will also help you establish the groundwork that will serve as a guide for your children as they grow up and start making decisions that will impact their lives.

While it is the dream of many people to be financially wealthy, it's important to remember that money is not the end. It is merely a means to allow you to do the things you want to do. By creating a solid financial footing, no matter how big or modest, you can eliminate many of the worries and challenges that confront many families on a daily basis and begin to provide a safe place in which your children's essential needs will be met.

Putting a Price Tag on the Priceless - The High Cost of Childhood

Perfection Unlimited

The Financial Facts of Life

On Your Mark, Get Set, Go!

From Pre-School to Behind the Wheel

Did You Say College?

So, Now What?

If you thought too much about the financial implications,

you wouldn't have children.

Imagine this scenario: Someone comes up to you, opens a briefcase full of money and says, "I'll give you $170,000 not to have a child."

What would you say? Would you be tempted?

A lump sum like that has its merits, but having a child provides you a wealth of joy, love, experience, personal growth and compassion that exceeds any dollar value. In simple terms, the experience of raising a child is priceless, and regardless of the cost, it can be one of life's greatest rewards.

Sentiment aside, the stark reality of raising a child is … *it isn't cheap*. And, while many parents will try to do it with minimal financial planning, the experience can be more rewarding with a well thought-out strategy.

- **PERFECTION UNLIMITED uncovers some of the perceived differences you may have between how other people raise their children and how you'll raise yours.**

- **THE FINANCIAL FACTS OF LIFE introduces you to what it costs, on average, to raise a family.**

- **ON YOUR MARK, GET SET, GO! takes a quick look at the expenses you can anticipate during baby's first year.**

- **FROM PRE-SCHOOL TO BEHIND THE WHEEL outlines some of the more common childhood expenses.**

- **DID YOU SAY COLLEGE? Explains just how much it costs to send a child to college.**

- **SO, NOW WHAT? Helps you take a deep breath and prepare to climb the financial mountain of parenthood.**

MONEY MATTERS

A recent USDA survey estimates the average cost of raising a child to age 17 is $170,000.

Perfection Unlimited

Before you had your own children, you knew other people's children. Some were accomplished, precious and polite. Others were ill-mannered, noisy, rude and uncontrollable.

Before you had your own children, you noticed what other people spent on their children. They bought expensive, adorable, designer baby clothes that looked generic the moment food stains covered them. And then, there's that huge toy car you would never buy for your three-year-old. You, of course, would never be so indulgent.

Your Imaginary Children

You imagined your own children as smart, curious, able to amuse themselves for hours by reading or playing quietly, yet always ready to go outside and catch a ball with you and the neighborhood kids. Your children would be as sensible as you are, not wanting any high-priced, materialistic items, preferring instead practical clothes and educational toys. And then … there's reality.

You miss out on so much if you don't have a family. I'm getting more of an education doing things with my kids than I got growing up.

Darlene, mother of three

Our Own Children

Things aren't always as we imagine. Our children are much more vibrant, independent and interesting than we ever could have predicted. They are much more engaging, insightful and creative than we ever could have dreamed. And, while raising them can be one of life's greatest rewards, it can also be much more challenging than we ever anticipated.

And often, more expensive.

Your children would be as sensible as you are, preferring practical clothes and educational toys.

Having kids is one of the most educational, exciting and thrilling experiences of my life. Who else could give me such great lessons in love, caring, compassion, commitment and playfulness, as well as time and money management?

Stephanie, mother of two

The Financial Facts of Life

When we decided we wanted to have children, we didn't take cost into consideration. We knew there would be expenses, we just didn't believe it had to be as expensive as everyone reports.

Jodi, mother of three

You need to stay on top of the business of running a family just like the head of a corporation does.

Today's chaotic world of fast-paced information, mounting consumerism and media bombardment makes your role as a parent far more than just taking care of food, clothing and shelter. You need to stay on top of the business of running a family just like the head of a corporation does. You are the Chief Financial Parent (CFP) of your household. And, as the CFP, you need to understand how to manage the financial obligations that come with raising a child.

Even before you had your first child, you got the honorary title of CFP. The moment you found out, "We're going to have a baby!" you had financial options to consider and financial decisions to make.

Many people become parents without thinking about the financial implications of raising a family. They assume they will somehow get by. These days, though, even the most practical and hard-working parents can easily find themselves in time crunches and money straits.

Let's take a look at the financial facts of life. Every year, a variety of government and independent agencies estimate what it costs to raise a child. A recent survey by the United States Department of Agriculture (USDA) estimated the cost of raising a child from birth to age 17 is more than $170,000 for a middle income family. This covers things such as:

- Housing
- Food
- Transportation
- Health care
- Child care
- Education
- Miscellaneous expenses like clothing, books or entertainment

Every year, a variety of government and independent agencies estimate what it costs to raise a child.

Many of you may be thinking – *"There has to be a way to raise a child for a lot less."* And you're right. Even with these rather daunting statistics, there are plenty of creative and innovative ways to control the cost of raising a child.

Some people measure their success by what they accomplish at work. I measure my success by what I accomplish at home. Managing our family's finances is a much greater challenge than managing our budgets at the office.

David, father of two

On Your Mark, Get Set, Go!

Children can be as expensive as you want them to be.

Steve, father of two

"What's the most expensive aspect of raising a child?" That's a question with more than one right answer. For most CFPs, the first child will be the most expensive. That's because:

- As new parents, you are more inclined to go overboard on your spending. You try to buy your infant the best of everything.

- Additional children can use the hand-me-downs of the first child (of course, if you have older nieces and nephews you might be able to use their hand-me-downs).

To put it in business terms, the start-up costs for any organization are always higher than the on-going maintenance.

When our daughter was born, I was shocked by how much the hospital bill was. Even though I knew there was no turning back, I asked my wife if our daughter would be repossessed if we didn't pay the bill. No matter what the cost, I'd never trade the experience of fatherhood for anything.

David, father of two

The first child can be the most expensive.

Baby's First Year

Have you ever been to a baby shower and wondered, "What is that contraption? Where will the mom put that? Does the baby really need all these things?" The number and variety of "things" available for a baby are practically endless. In fact, with all the choices available to new parents, it's not hard to get carried away when you're shopping.

With that in mind, it's easy to understand how some parents spend $7,000 to $10,000 for such things as baby furniture, clothes, formula, child care, diapers, medicines and doctor's visits during a baby's first year.

While the list of adorable furniture, clothes and accessories is endless, the list of what you actually need is a little less daunting:

- Baby clothes
- Formula or food supplements
- Crib
- Diapers
- Stroller
- Car seat
- High chair
- Medical care

Other first year expenses can include:

- Child care
- Portable play pen
- Furniture and toys

You try to buy

your infant

the best

of everything.

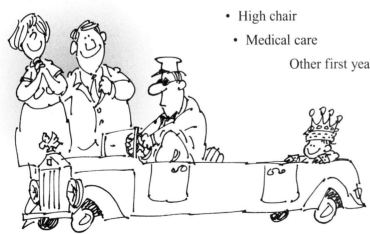

CFP TIP *Cross-Train Your Baby Furniture*

I was shocked when I learned that nursery furniture costs as much as living room furniture. So we thought ahead. We purchased a crib that could later convert into a full size double bed. We bought a changing table that converted into a desk. Even though the furniture was expensive, we looked at it as an investment we would use for a long period of time.
Darlene, mother of three

From Pre-School to Behind the Wheel

I was surprised by the cost of having kids. Especially as the kids got older and more involved in activities and sports.
Kelly, mother of three

Just when the earaches end and the child care expenses taper off, extra activities and socializing begin. For some parents, this marks the start of an era that includes:

- Nicer clothes
- School expenses
- Before and after-school care
- Fees for extracurricular sports and other activities
- Birthday parties, movies and shopping malls
- Summer camps
- Cell phones, computers and more

"We purchased a crib that could later convert into a full size double bed. We bought a changing table that converted into a desk."

The types of expenses you choose will tie in with your values and your financial goals (we explore this in more detail in Chapter Two).

This can also be a time of intense peer pressure, for both the parents and the child. Your kids will compare their situation to "other families" who may have more and better houses, clothes, vacations and entertainment options.

MONEY MATTERS

According to surveys,

as children get older,

they also get

more expensive.

When we had our first child, we lived in a one-bedroom apartment. It was all we could afford. Looking back, I'm glad we didn't have the money to move. Living in such a small space really brought the family together. I loved hearing my son sleep while I was falling asleep.

Jack, father of three

As your children get older, you may have to find some creative ways to deal with some of the financial demands and scheduling issues that come with raising them.

Here are a few stories from parents who have dealt with these issues.

Flexing Your Time and Saving Your Money

Gwen worked days and her husband, Tom, worked from 3:00 in the afternoon to 11:00 at night, with lots of overtime. He was asleep when their son went to school and at work when their son came home (that meant they didn't see each other very often). It also meant they were spending money for after-school care. Plus, Gwen was being worn down by taking care of all of the household responsibilities.

After a lot of conversation and searching for alternatives, they decided Tom would switch to the 11:00 pm-7:00 am shift. This helped the family save after-school care money and it meant they could spend more time together.

The change in work hours transformed their family life. Now, Tom is home after school and able to take their son to karate and music classes. Plus, he also has time to do grocery shopping, which turns out to be another money saver.

"He thought I spent too much on groceries," Gwen says. "This works out great for me, because I don't like to grocery shop. He plans out the menus for the week and shops, and I cook."

Action at the Auction: The Earn-Your-Own-Toys-Plan

Jodi's sons wanted a basketball hoop. "I told them we couldn't afford to buy a basketball hoop," Jodi says. "I suggested they gather together all the toys and games they weren't using and sell them."

They went through their things and within four weeks they made $185, just by going to an on-line auction and selling the things they no longer wanted.

"They were thrilled by the process," Jodi says.

Jodi did the computer work. The whole family got involved, checking to see how the bidding was going. Once the items sold, the boys had the job of packing everything and addressing the shipments.

Now the family has a system for saving unused toys for future sales.

 CFP TIP   *Selling Lessons On-Line*

The on-line auction experience gives kids a chance to get into the marketplace without leaving home. The family can talk about values and the costs associated with buying and selling. Plus, there's the element of excitement and the thrill of earning money.

We gathered all the toys and games they weren't using and sold them.

The Birth of the Small Party

Children's birthday parties have grown more elaborate and more expensive. Twenty kids bowling and having snacks. Fifteen kids going to an indoor playground. The whole class going for pizza and video games. Parents often feel trapped into keeping up and making sure their child doesn't feel "left out."

"What used to be a fun and simple family gathering now turns me into a super party planner," says one parent. "I agonize over what we can do that the kids haven't already done. And these kids are only seven years old!"

Kelly came up with a solution. "One big party every three years," she told her son. On the other years, he can have a couple friends over to hang out, play games, spend the night and celebrate in the old fashioned way.

For Kelly, that decision has not only saved her money, time and stress, but it has also given her practice in asserting her values in a world filled with peer pressures.

"I agonize over what we can do that the kids haven't already done."

$ CFP TIP   *Planning a Budget-Friendly Party*

Instead of treating party guests to a movie and dinner at a restaurant, try having a sleepover with craft projects and let the kids make or decorate the cake.

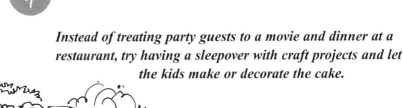

One-Activity-a-Semester Plan

Marie wants well-rounded children. Every night she drives them to various lessons. If you want to talk to Marie in the evening, try her cell phone. Then be prepared for the background noise of tap dancing, basketball bouncing, karate yells and play rehearsals.

For some parents, an activity-packed lifestyle really works. For other parents, time and money are limited commodities. That's why Annie came up with the one-activity-a-semester plan. Her daughters choose one thing they really want to do each semester. For Annie, this reduces the financial stress of paying for endless lessons and also the emotional and physical requirement of driving all evening, eating on the run and feeling like there is no quiet time to connect with her kids.

From Car Talk to Leaving High School

The high school years can often be as expensive as, if not more expensive than, your baby's first year. Especially if you decide to buy your child a car.

This can be both a rewarding and maddening time for you. On one hand, your child, who looks more like an adult every day, is old enough to get a job, earn his own money and drive himself around. This eliminates a lot of the transportation burden you may have experienced during the previous 16 years. On the other hand, the costs associated with having a job and being able to drive can far outweigh the benefits. In addition, your child still has the basic needs of room, board (some people will swear their kids' food consumption triples during this time) and clothing. Add to this the costs associated with school dances, class trips, peer pressure and, dare we say it, preparing for college. Once you put it all together, it's easy to see how expensive it can be to raise a teenager.

The teen years are a time to work with your kids and encourage them to become financially aware. This is also the time to partner with your children to help them discover the true costs of adulthood.

Here are some of the financial issues that often come up:

- Car – insurance, maintenance and gasoline

- Personal computers

- Clothes

Be prepared for the background noise of tap dancing, basketball bouncing, karate yells and play rehearsals.

- Cell phones
- Travel and entertainment
- School activities, such as trips, dances and sporting events
- This can also be a period of life when temptation appears in the form of a credit card, or two

As we shared in *Yes, You Can! Raise Financially Aware Kids*, be open with your kids about your own financial limitations and how much you can afford to contribute. Also, talk through your expectations, so your children don't get carried away with all work and no studying.

We always gave our son an allowance. However, when he was old enough to work, his allowance covered only his expenses during the school year. During the summer, when his earning potential was far greater than the allowance we were paying, we told him if he wanted money, he needed to get a job. He accepted the challenge and started working at the neighborhood grocery store. We allowed him to continue to work during the school year, provided he maintained his grades. He's a high school senior now and has had a part-time job for the past four years. Each new job he takes gives him more responsibility and experience he'll use to support himself as an adult.

David, father of two

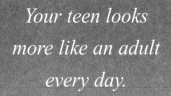

Your teen looks more like an adult every day.

Did You Say College?

You need a pair of binoculars to keep track of the rising college costs. Historically, college costs have risen an average of about 5% a year.

As of 2003, the four-year cost for a public in-state school (including room, board and books) is around $56,000; out-of-state is $83,000; and, private school is $120,000. That means if your child was born this year, college could cost anywhere from $135,000 to more than $287,000.

Now, take a deep breath and when you're ready, turn to our college chapter in Part II for some creative ways to prepare for this expense.

So, Now What?

The purpose of this chapter is to introduce you to the financial mountain that's ahead of you. In the following chapters we'll help you start climbing the mountain so you can reach the top as painlessly as possible. **All it takes is determination and a willingness to stay focused on your priorities.**

As your family's CFP, you know that raising a child requires more than just financial management: you have to be an expert in child psychology, accounting, resource allocation, event planning, time management and conflict resolution. While the experience of raising your kids may pull you in many directions and tug heavily at your purse strings, the trade-off in love, joy and fulfillment far outweighs the cost.

...the experience of raising your kids may pull you in many directions...

Taking the First Step - Determine Your Priorities

What Values are Most Important to You in Raising Your Family?

What Does Money Mean to You?

Money Talks

Understanding Your Priorities

Where are You Now?

Your values will stick with your kids as you launch them on their own.

Most of us have an idea of what we think makes a good parent. This list might include a certain amount of time we should spend with our kids, a certain set of behaviors we want our children to emulate and expectations, experiences and dreams we have for our children's future. We use this list to decide how best to raise our family.

This idea also represents the goals and values that are the bottom line of parenting. These are the principles and values we cannot afford to compromise.

In this chapter, you will see the importance of establishing your values and how to use them to keep your family's financial goals in sight. Here are some of the topics you'll explore:

- **WHAT VALUES ARE MOST IMPORTANT TO YOU IN RAISING YOUR FAMILY?** provides a framework for using your money by helping you discover what's really important to you.

- **WHAT DOES MONEY MEAN TO YOU?** encourages you to see how your attitudes about money were formed by your family history.

- **MONEY TALKS** helps you talk to your kids about money.

- **UNDERSTANDING YOUR PRIORITIES** gives you food for thought when it comes to saving for retirement, college and vacation. It also helps you define a strategy for sharing your time and resources.

- **WHERE ARE YOU NOW?** introduces you to the importance of finding harmony in your parenting priorities, family values and financial dreams.

What Values are Most Important to You in Raising Your Family?

It doesn't matter to me how much money we have. What matters is how we use that money. Money can tear a family apart if it's not properly managed or kept in perspective.

Ayeesha, mother of two

Unfortunately, some adults believe that money is the primary, if not the only, source of happiness. In order to be happy, they believe they need a lot of money. These parents either knowingly or unknowingly pass that belief on to their kids.

Most of us don't believe that money is the basis for happiness. However, money is important in providing those things your family needs or wants.

What could be difficult about having that much money?

Before you can build a financial foundation that supports you in raising your family, it is important to understand what's really important to you and your family. These are your family's values.

To begin, discuss this question with the entire family.

"What if we had all the money we wanted?"

Then ask each family member:

- How much do you want?

- Why did you pick that amount?

- How would your life be better tomorrow if you had that money?

Now get specific:

- If you had all the money you wanted, what would you do differently?

- What could be difficult about having that much money?

- What are some of the things that couldn't be bought, even if you had all the money you wanted?

Finally:

- Assume you had to give back everything you were able to buy or do with the money except for one thing – what one item or experience would you keep?

- Why did you pick that item?

- If you could keep two, what would be second?

- How would you prioritize your top five things or experiences? Why did you prioritize them this way?

This is a great dinner table conversation. Doing this exercise can help you and your family quickly get to the core of what's really important in your life.

Continue your family dialogue by discussing how each of you would most like to live your life by answering these questions:

- How do I want to be remembered?

- Do I want people to know me by what I own or by who I am?

- What sacrifices am I willing to make in order to create my own success?

Your answers to these questions will provide a basis for setting other goals, making financial decisions and establishing your priorities.

Eating dinner can be a learning experience.

Finally, examine how your family currently spends money to see how your purchases mesh with what you want to accomplish. This is a direct reflection of your family's values. To help you get started, review this list and consider how these activities or items fit in with your family values and financial priorities. Write a number next to each item listed below based on its importance to the family:

10 New car
4 Big house
7 Sharing with others
1 Enhanced relationships with others
8 Newest computer, TV and/or video system
9 Fun things for the kids
3 College savings
___ Donations
5 Family vacations
2 Retirement savings
6 Entertainment
___ Other _____

The way you prioritize these activities provides some insight into your family's value system relative to how you spend your money.

How your kids look at money depends on how you look at it.

Decide what you want most. Prioritize your wants and then create a plan that meets your priorities. If you are determined to become financially independent, it is really quite simple: Spend less than you earn, or make more than you spend and wisely invest the difference. Try your best at whatever you choose to do.

James Stowers

What Does Money Mean to You?

Money has a place and purpose in each family. As your family's CFP, you are your children's primary source of financial information. How your kids look at money will depend a great deal on how you look at money.

Money is more than just a means of exchange. Some believe money is one of the means to happiness; if only they had enough of it, life would be perfect. Money can be accumulated or spent, depending on your priorities. Money can give you a sense of security, but at the same time the pursuit of money can keep you away from what you value and love most … your family.

Take advantage of this opportunity to explore and define the role money plays in your life. Talk about your money beliefs and history with your family.

Here is an exercise to help you explore how your childhood experiences and money stories affect your current financial attitudes. The more you understand the principles you learned growing up, both spoken and implied, the better your chances of defining your own family's values.

What ancestral money habits did you inherit?

Consider your answers to the following questions:

- What are your family money stories? Include the hardships family members may have endured and their financial successes.

- Were your ancestors business owners or did they work for others?

- What money stories did you hear from or about your grandparents?

- What stories did your parents tell you about the cost of living when they were growing up?

- What advice, warnings or rules did you absorb from listening to family stories about money?

- What money-oriented advice did your parents give you?

- What did your parents' actions show you about money?

- What ancestral money habits did you inherit?

Once you've explored your past generation's money stories and beliefs, consider how those attitudes affect you and your family today. Remember, your children are watching you and learning from your example. It's important to understand your own money values because your children absorb these same values every day.

 CFP TIP   *Firming Up Finances*

Some people review their financial goals every year at tax time to make certain they are still spending money in meaningful ways.

Money Talks

Many parents agree that talking with their kids about money is easier than talking about sex. But it's hard to get the conversation started. We are too busy, we don't want to worry our kids and we really don't know what to say or when to say it.

However, if you don't talk to your children about money, you may send them out into the consumer world unprepared.

The trick is to make the money conversation fun, energizing and interesting.

The good news is that kids are curious about money. Wouldn't it be a great start to share with them your values and financial goals? You can then ask them what their goals are, too. You may be amazed at how much you have in common.

Here are some general tips for money **TALKS**:

Talk to your kids about money as early as possible. Letting young children pay for something with a dollar bill will help give them the idea that those green things in their parent's wallet mean something.

Act casually. Make money just another conversational topic, like sports, the weekly activity schedule or what's for dinner.

Leave money in its proper place. Don't let it dominate your value system.

Know your audience. Direct your conversation about money to each child's age and interest. Draw your children into a talk about money in a way that is meaningful to them. Use stories from your own life.

Sprinkle questions throughout your conversation and listen carefully to the answers. Everyone loves attention. Your questions and attentive listening give your children a sense of acceptance and deepen your family bond.

Understanding Your Priorities

Most families share four common financial goals. They are: retirement, college, vacation and sharing with others. In this section, you'll have the opportunity to look at each of these in detail to better define your expectations for each goal.

Take some time to think about the following priority questions. If you're married, compare your answers with your spouse's to see where you are compatible, where your priorities differ and how you can work better as a team to reach your goals. If you're single, try to understand the reason you answered the way you did and how the way you think about money affects your life.

Retirement

I don't ever want to be dependent on my children, so saving for retirement is very important to me. I put aside an amount every month, no matter what.

Vanetta, mother of two

How can you work better as a team to reach your goals?

The word "retirement" may mean very different things to different people. No matter how you define it, asking these questions can make planning for your retirement easier:

- How do you define retirement?

- Do you plan to retire? At what age?

- If married, does your spouse plan to retire? At what age?

- Where will you live? How will you pay for your residence?

- How will you occupy your days?

- Are you taking advantage of a retirement plan at work?

- Do you have a savings or investment plan outside of work?

- What sources of income do you have to fund your retirement?

- What is your back-up plan if your initial plans take a detour?

Paying for Your Kids' College Education

For many families, education is a top priority. With it, a child can excel in many areas. Without it, a child runs the risk of limiting their career and social opportunities. Many parents want their child to attend college, but they never discuss how they are going to pay for it ... *until it's too late.*

Our biggest financial goal is making certain our kids have enough money for college. Even though our children are young, that goal is primary in our minds.

Kelly, mother of three

> *The time to start making college plans is when your child is born.*

The time to start making college plans is when your child is born. In doing so, it's important to decide how you will pay for this education. Some of the key issues to discuss include:

- How much of your kid's total college cost (room, board, tuition and expenses) do you intend, or hope, to pay for?

- Do you want your child to attend public or private college?

- How much can you save on a regular basis toward achieving this goal?

- How will inflation affect your savings plan?

- If money becomes tight, are you willing to use this money to pay for family expenses or is this money only for education?

- If your child doesn't go to college, what will happen to the money?

- What sort of savings vehicle will you use – UGMA (Uniform Gift to Minors Act), 529 Plan, Savings Account or ROTH IRA? Do you understand the benefits and consequences of each option?

Although these questions seem simple enough, many people do not discuss or analyze how they feel about these important issues. Talking about money is one of the keys to harmony in a family.

We are saving for our kids' education, but we don't know how much we'll be able to help them through college. My parents did not help me, and I made it. We don't believe we have to pay their whole way through college.

Susan, mother of two

In Section II, we provide some very specific information that will help you put your college savings plan into action.

How will inflation affect your savings plan?

Vacation

While a vacation may seem like a luxury to some, others consider it a necessity. Answer the following questions to determine how vacations fit into your values:

- Do you feel that vacations are important?

- How do vacations fit into your priorities?

- How do you hope your children will benefit from a vacation?

- Can you afford to go on a vacation?

- For you, are vacations strictly for relaxation, or will they include work?

- For your kids, are vacations strictly for "fun," or will they include opportunities for education?

- How often should you take a family vacation?

- How long should a vacation last?

- What is your idea of an ideal vacation destination?

- What is the best way to travel on vacation?

- If you saved money for a family vacation and then decided not to go, what would you do with the money? Based on how you answered this question, which is more important to you, the family vacation or the other things you'd do with the money?

- If you didn't go on a "vacation," how else could you give your family a similar experience?

Are vacations strictly for relaxation, or will they include work?

Sharing with Others

Besides spending, saving and investing money, another choice is to donate money to your favorite causes. As you talk about the following questions, include your kids in the dialogue. This is a great opportunity to introduce them to the concepts of sharing and giving back to the community (even if you can't make a financial donation, you may want to consider sharing your time).

- Why do we want to give?

- What do we like about giving?

- What causes do we feel strongly about?

- What charities do we want to know more about?

- What issues do we think need our support and help?

- Do we know anyone who's involved in those charities or issues?

- Will we give time, money or material goods?

How Much is Enough?

Can you ever have enough? For us, it's a matter of identifying our priorities. Since we've had a family, our priorities have changed. Both my husband and I work, but our careers aren't our priority. The size of our house and the type of cars we drive aren't important. Vacations are not important. For us, it's difficult to continue to pursue those things and successfully raise our family in a stress-free environment. When we first became parents, we didn't know this. We learned it as we went along.

Jodi, mother of three

> MONEY MATTERS
>
> *When parents solve a problem that appears to be money-related, they may also reduce stress and improve their family life.*

Where are You Now?

Think about your financial priorities. How do they fit in with your family values and parenting priorities? Are your priorities the same as your spouse's? If not, are the two sets of goals and dreams working together?

You may find inconsistencies between your values and the way you are using your money. For example, if financial security is one of your values, but instead of investing you've been spending most of your income to buy clothes and eat out, your use of money is inconsistent with your values. When your values are inconsistent with your spending, it's much harder to live a happy, fulfilling life.

In the next chapter, we will show you how to look at your spending and organize your finances. This exercise will help you put a framework around how you're using money and how your financial values are supporting your family values.

You may find inconsistencies between your values and the way you are using your money.

NOTES

Where Does Your Money Go?

Imagine if you stopped and thought about each dollar

you handed over at the coffee shop...

I n Chapter Two, you identified your financial values and determined your priorities. This chapter will help you learn even more about how you and your family think about money. In addition to helping you find ways to spend less than you earn, this chapter will also provide information on:

- **TRACKING THE WANDERING DOLLAR introduces the concept that, in order to meet your financial goals, you need to understand how you spend your money.**

- **GETTING ORGANIZED: THE ULTIMATE MONEY ORDER explains how having an organized bill payment system can save you money, ease stress and help improve your financial position.**

- **TAMING THE WILD EXPENSES: DEVELOPING A BUDGET gives you the tools you need to understand the flow of your money.**

- **CLOSING THE GAP BETWEEN INCOME AND EXPENSES demonstrates how, by spending less, earning more or doing both, you can make certain you have money left over at the end of the month.**

- **TIME, MONEY AND *DETERMINATION* points out some creative ways to trim the fat in your expenses.**

Tracking the Wandering Dollar

Whether it's a quarter someone dropped in a grocery store parking lot or a $10 bill in the pocket of some slacks you haven't worn for months, everyone loves the surprise of finding a little extra money.

However, most of us don't like the surprise of "misplacing" money – that $20 we had yesterday which has mysteriously disappeared today. Where did it go? Well, there was the two dollars for your morning coffee, five dollars for lunch, four dollars for your kid's lunch, one dollar for gum, five dollars for a magazine and three dollars for that "gotta have it" toy in the check-out line.

Imagine if you stopped and thought about each dollar you handed over at the coffee shop or lovingly gave to your kids. Would you rather spend $40 on double mocha lattes every month or use that same money to help pay for a family vacation?

Only you know the right answer. You might really enjoy and want those lattes. They may be a way for you to socialize. Or they may simply be a habit, your way of getting through the morning. Regardless of why you spend your money the way you do, you need to understand the reasons behind your spending decisions. In doing so, you can start to track the wandering dollar and use your money to fulfill your future.

> *We kept a daily record of how we spent our money. This included the cost of every item and specifically what it was for. At the end of the month, we looked at the list and asked:* **Did we get our money's worth? Are we satisfied with the way we spent our money?** *If we answered "no" to either question on a particular item, we focused on the negative aspect of the experience and vowed never to repeat the mistake. By doing this, we eliminated some expenses and found extra money to* **invest and save for the things we really wanted to do.**
>
> James Stowers

"We kept a daily record of how we spent our money."

For some people, keeping track of how money is spent is an easy process. For others, it's a chore that can quickly become a struggle as the demands of parenthood, work and home increase.

The Espresso Bandit

I don't like to think too much about money. When my wife convinced me that we needed to create a budget, I wasn't sure I wanted to. But I agreed to try it for a week. At the end of the week, I could see how my double espresso, lottery tickets and miscellaneous expenses added up.

It was several hundred dollars each month. That's money I wasn't even conscious of spending.

Darren, father of two

For some, keeping track of how they spend money is easy.

Darren's story illustrates how watching expenses can open your eyes to how you think about and spend money. It's also a key that unlocks the door to more financial freedom.

 CFP TIP   *The Budget Revisited*

If you already have a budget, take a little time and compare your values and goals with your current plan. Make sure that your money and your dreams work together.

Getting Organized: The Ultimate Money Order

...keep your bills where you can see them as a constant reminder.

We have a "family meeting" once a week to plan menus and discuss any major purchases we are considering. Our daughter is expected to come to these meetings, although she doesn't like them. She says they're boring. But we believe that having her participate in our money management conversations will make her more financially aware as she gets older.

Pam, mother of one

All families should have a method of organizing their finances. In some homes, one parent is in charge of bill paying and money decisions. In others, the parents work as a team and divide responsibilities according to their interests and abilities. Yet, in other families, the parents stay organized by having separate checking accounts and dividing up different types of expenses. To stay on track, no matter how you do it, consider the following four-step method.

Four Steps to Getting and Staying Organized

STEP 1 Organize your bills as they come in. Have a designated place where you put your incoming bills. Whether it's a filing folder, a basket or the corner of a desk, keep them where you can see them as a constant reminder.

STEP 2 Pay your bills regularly and on time. This helps you plan your monthly expenses and avoid late charges.

STEP 3 Track your expenses. Develop a system, either on paper or with a computer, that allows you to see where your money is going.

STEP 4 Review your expenses. On a monthly basis, sit down and take an honest look at how you've spent your money. Then decide if you're getting your money's worth.

In our home, I manage all the household bills. When a bill comes in, I write the amount on the envelope and the date I plan to pay it. I put the bills in order by payment date in a file on my desk. I file the ordinary bills horizontally and the large bills, such as insurance and mortgage, vertically. The vertical bills stick out and alert me that I have a large payment coming up and the family needs to be careful about how we spend money. It's a simple and visual system.

David, father of two

My husband used to pay all the bills until he started getting late charges. That irritated me and it irritated him. Now I pay the bills and put the information into a money management computer program. This system helps keep both our finances and our relationship on track.

Francie, mother of two

My husband pays the bills. That's because when I was doing it, I got stressed out worrying about money. When he volunteered to take over, I was relieved. Even though I know how much we spend, not seeing those bills every month makes me calmer.

Elaine, mother of two

MONEY MATTERS

By being organized, you can avoid late charges. Which, for some credit cards, can be $35 ... or more.

Taming the Wild Expenses: Developing a Budget

In order to spend less than you earn, you need to create a spending plan or budget. A good budget is simple, flexible and easy to track. Here's what you need to look at to develop a budget.

Income. What money is coming your way? This includes regular income from work and investments. List only the income that's certain.

Expenses. How do you spend your money? Create a list with all your expense categories. Start with the regular monthly bills, then create categories for all the variable expenses you can think of, such as car upkeep, groceries, donations and entertainment. To help you get organized, it may be helpful to review your check register and credit card statements from the previous year.

The more categories you list, the more likely you are to really understand where your money goes.

 CFP TIP   *Use Your Budget to Have More Fun*

One family noticed it spent only $50 for all entertainment during the month. "To me, that meant we were not getting out enough," the mom said. "So we cut our expenses in a different area so we could spend more on entertainment and family activities outside the house. That brought the family closer together and reinforced one of our values."

Here is a chart that can help you develop your budget and track your cash flow. Copy this onto a separate sheet of paper or into a computer spreadsheet program. You can also download a ready-made spreadsheet from the Resource Library on the Stowers Innovations Web site at www.stowers-innovations.com.

	JAN	FEB	MAR	APR	MAY	JUN	JUL	AUG	SEP	OCT	NOV	DEC	**TOTAL**
INCOME:													
SALARY													
INVESTMENTS													
OTHER													
TOTAL INCOME													
EXPENSES:													
SHELTER:													
MORTGAGE PAYMENTS													
PROPERTY TAXES													
INSURANCE													
PERSONAL PROPERTY TAXES													

	JAN	FEB	MAR	APR	MAY	JUN	JUL	AUG	SEP	OCT	NOV	DEC	**TOTAL**
AUTOMOTIVE:													
CAR PAYMENTS													
CAR INSURANCE													
FUEL													
OIL CHANGES													
OTHER REPAIR AND MAINTENANCE													
HOUSEHOLD EXPENSES:													
GROCERIES – FOOD													
GROCERIES – HOUSEHOLD GOODS													
GROCERIES – PETS													
CLOTHING, ADULT													
APPLIANCES, REPAIR/REPLACEMENT													
UTILITIES:													
WATER													
GAS													
ELECTRIC													
INTERNET													
PHONE													

	JAN	FEB	MAR	APR	MAY	JUN	JUL	AUG	SEP	OCT	NOV	DEC	**TOTAL**
CABLE													
LAWN COSTS													
PEST CONTROL													
ALARM SYSTEM													
GARBAGE/ RECYCLING													
HEALTH AND LIFE:													
PRESCRIPTIONS													
DENTAL													
DOCTOR													
HEALTH CARE INSURANCE													
LIFE INSURANCE													
GLASSES/CONTACTS													
PET VETERINARIAN													
OTHER													
KID COSTS:													
EDUCATION													
DAY CARE													
AFTER SCHOOL CARE													

	JAN	FEB	MAR	APR	MAY	JUN	JUL	AUG	SEP	OCT	NOV	DEC	**TOTAL**
ENTERTAINMENT													
LESSONS, ACTIVITIES, SPORTS													
CLOTHING													
SCHOOL LUNCHES													
ALLOWANCE													
WORK RELATED COSTS:													
EATING OUT													
COFFEE, PASTRY													
BUS/TRAIN FARE													
CO-WORKER OUTINGS AND GIFTS													
PERSONAL EXPENSES:													
MAKE-UP, TOILETRIES													
HAIRCUTS													
DRY CLEANING													
BIRTHDAY PRESENTS													
ANNIVERSARY PRESENTS													
HOLIDAY PRESENTS													

	JAN	FEB	MAR	APR	MAY	JUN	JUL	AUG	SEP	OCT	NOV	DEC	**TOTAL**
BOOKS													
VACATION													
EATING OUT													
CONCERTS, THEATER													
MOVIES													
VIDEO RENTAL													
OTHER ENTERTAINMENT													
MONTHLY DEPOSITS:													
COLLEGE FUND													
RETIREMENT FUND													
EMERGENCY RESERVE													
INVESTMENTS													
OTHER SAVINGS													
TOTAL EXPENSES													
DIFFERENCE INCOME - EXPENSE													

Putting Yourself On Spending Detail

Once you've created your categories, keep track of all your spending. For some people, it is tempting to ignore the little expenses – a pack of gum, a magazine, bottled water – but they do add up and it's worth your while to jot them down and include them.

At the end of the month, return to your budget and fill in the blanks. Add in any categories you left out of the plan. See if all the expenses make sense to you. Where do you spend too much? Are you supporting your values and goals through the way you spend your money? Are you saving for college and investing in your retirement in a way that reflects your priorities?

As you review your monthly expenses, answer these questions:

- Are you happy with the way you spent your money?

- Did you get your money's worth?

- Were there any unanticipated expenses?

- Did you spend your money on things you don't remember?

- If you had the month to live over, would you spend your money the same way?

- Are there things you wish you had done, but couldn't because you didn't have enough money?

- What expenses can you anticipate for next month? Are you ready for them?

Organizing Your Money and Strengthening Your Relationship

After months of worrying about money and bickering when it came time to pay bills, we decided to create a budget. As we compared our income and expenses, we realized just how lucky we are. At the end of the month, we have money to save and invest for our future. Creating a budget helped us understand our financial position. It also reduced our money worries, which brought us closer together. Now we don't get stressed out every month by how much we're spending. Instead, we find pleasure in how much we're saving.

Roseanne, mother of two

 CFP TIP   *Training New Money Managers*

As your children get older, help them develop a budget. If they get an allowance or work for money, show them ways to save and spend wisely. Many kids who eagerly spend their parent's money become much more frugal when they start spending their own money.

*Keep track of **all** spending.*

Everywhere you go, the consumer world is beckoning you. The sight of the sparkling, new cars on an automobile dealer's lot makes you yearn for something new. You drop off your child to play with one of his friends. and their big home makes you wish you could buy something "bigger and nicer" for your family. You sit in the privacy of your home, and a barrage of TV commercials tries to convince you to spend, spend, SPEND!

It's hard not to pay attention or be influenced by the commercial messages around you. It's even harder staying focused on your long-term financial goals so you are able to do what's really important to you.

Watch Your Step

I want us to feel good about the financial choices we make. So we try to avoid being influenced by consumerism and social status and distinguish between wants and needs.

Darlene, mother of three

Closing the Gap Between Income and Expenses

Sometimes, no matter how hard you try, you may find that your expenses exceed your income. Closing the gap between expenses and earning can be like losing those extra ten pounds. It seems like it should be so easy and yet somehow, it's such a struggle.

Spend Less, Earn More or Do Both

It sounds simple enough … spend less than you earn. But in practice, it can be very challenging.

So how do you turn it around so your income exceeds your expenses? There are three ways:

- Spend less

- Earn more

- Do both

Your decision depends on your circumstances and values. For example, no matter how fiercely Jodi and her husband cut expenses, no matter how rigidly they followed their budget, they could not seem to get by on one income.

"The numbers added up when we did our initial budget. But in reality, extra expenses kept creeping in. We were falling behind by at least $200 a month. We had to decide where we could cut our expenses or find a way to earn more money," Jodi said.

They analyzed their priorities. They wanted their kids to have lots of parental attention. That's why Jodi quit working outside the home. But they also wanted to continue to live the same lifestyle and save money. So they decided to try to find a way to increase their income. Jodi had a marketable skill and tried her hand at consulting.

"My husband and I developed a schedule that allowed us to spend the time we wanted with the kids and still both work."

She was able to generate enough business each month to cover their "extra" expenses. Over the years, she built her business. And, when her boys went to school, she took advantage of the extra free time to expand her business.

Doing Two Things at Once

Susan didn't know how her family would make it to the end of the month without going into debt or dipping into the family savings account. She planned her food budget to the penny. She turned down the thermostat and told the kids they'd have to go without movie rentals and carry-out pizza. Even with all the trimming, she couldn't make ends meet. She struggled with how she could still be a stay-at-home mom and earn a little extra money. Then a friend called and asked Susan if she'd help make bridesmaid dresses.

"Of course," Susan said.

Her friend brought over the material and asked Susan how much she would charge.

"Nothing," Susan said. "I enjoy sewing."

"I'm paying you," her friend insisted.

The amount her friend paid was enough for Susan to buy a new sewing machine and still have some extra money to pay bills. The new sewing machine made her job easier and gave her the confidence to offer her services to other people. Soon, several of the bridesmaids brought their dresses over for alterations. Susan had stumbled into a small business. The money she earned from her business helped her family regain its financial footing.

> ### MONEY MATTERS
>
> *Since 1994, an annual average of 5.5% of employed people have had more than one job.*
>
> 2001, Bureau of Labor Statistics

Pinching the Budget

Expenses had gotten out of hand at Pat's household. They'd recently moved, and the move seemed to swallow increasing amounts of money. Pat and her husband vowed to cut expenses.

They looked carefully at their budget. They talked about expenses with some of their frugal friends and asked for advice. They held a family meeting and asked their children for their ideas.

After six months of watching expenses, we got back on track.

"Talking about it reduced the embarrassment I felt at not being able to live on our income," says Pat. "The more I opened up and asked for advice, the more I learned what a common issue this was."

After six months of closely watching their spending, Pat's family got back on track.

"And we plan to stay that way!" says Pat.

Time, Money and DETERMINATION

A lot of people struggle with living from paycheck to paycheck and getting further into debt each month. This is a time to remember your duty as a CFP and your power as a financially literate adult. Take a look at how you're spending your time and money. As one parent put it, "I am constantly trying to balance between time and money."

Start by looking again at your budget. Are there areas where you could get items cheaper or free? Are there things you are buying now that you could barter or trade for with someone else? Do you really need cable TV or two phone lines? Can you work a part-time job on weekends or evenings? How determined are you to make your long-term financial dreams a reality?

Here are some ideas:

My daughter is wearing clothes sent to her by her cousin in Israel. When my uncle retired he sent me all his barely worn suits and ties. They are just my size. When we visit my wife's sister and brother, we almost always take clothes for their kids that our kids no longer wear. By being open to hand-me-downs, our immediate and extended families have saved hundreds, possibly thousands of dollars on clothes.

David, father of two

When our kids say, "Why can't we go out to eat more often? Why can't we go to the amusement park?" we tell them that we make a certain amount of money and it has to cover all our needs, including food, clothing and shelter. We talk about our expenses and ask them which they'd rather have, a house to live in with electricity and running water or pizza and games at the restaurant down the street. This type of comparison helps them understand.

Jodi, mother of three

We have never bought any furniture. We have only hand-me-downs. Our house is eclectic and we like it that way. Plus, we've saved lots of money and made our friends and relatives happy by giving their used furniture a second home.

Tiffany, mother of two.

> *By being open to hand-me-downs, our family has saved hundreds.*

CFP TIP　*Buy and Buy*

Involve your kids in the buying decisions. It's fun to talk through what are your needs and wants and think of possible alternatives. You may get some great ideas from your kids while teaching them to think before they buy.

In this chapter, you've analyzed your monthly expenses and looked at how your budget and your priorities can work together. In the next chapter, you'll look at where your money comes from and some of the hidden expenses of earning an income.

"We have never bought any furniture."

NOTES

The Price of Employment

Values vs. Income - The Big Balancing Act

What's My Salary Really Worth?

Income Reduction – Living on Less

One Plus: Bridging the Earnings Gap

...trying to balance between time and money...

Now that you know where your money goes, let's take a look at where your money comes from. For most of us, this will be easy to answer … we have to work for our income. What you may not realize is that the costs associated with work may outweigh the benefits.

In this chapter, we'll show you ways to analyze how much that hard-earned money is really worth to you.

- **VALUES VS. INCOME – THE BIG BALANCING ACT. One of your primary jobs as a CFP is maintaining your family's values in a way that is meaningful and satisfying while balancing how you spend your time and money.**

- **WHAT'S MY SALARY REALLY WORTH? You know how much you earn, but how much does it cost you? Take a look at some of the expenses that can reduce the worth of your salary.**

- **INCOME REDUCTION – LIVING ON LESS. Thinking of changing from a two-income family to one? If so, here are some suggestions and tips from those who have made the switch.**

- **ONE PLUS: BRIDGING THE EARNINGS GAP. Small jobs on the side can help fill in the gaps.**

Values vs. Income – The Big Balancing Act

Whether they work outside of the home or are stay-at-home parents, many parents feel they don't have enough time or enough money. Sometimes both!

Stay-at-home parents may think all of their family's wants would be resolved if they had additional income.

"During your life, you will earn a sizable fortune. Regardless of how much you earn, only what you save is really yours."

James Stowers

Working parents sometimes feel that, because of the amount of time they spend at their jobs, they don't have as much time as they would like to dedicate to their relationships with their children and spouse.

As a CFP, one of your primary jobs is to make sure you maintain your family's values in a way that is meaningful and satisfying, while still finding the right balance between time and money. The trick is finding that spot at which the balance feels right for you and your family.

How you answer the following questions will help you identify the balance point for your family:

How much time do I want to spend with my family?

- How much time do I want to spend with my family?

- Where do I find the greatest satisfaction:
  - earning an income to provide for my family; or,
  - being at home with my family and taking care of their needs?

- What are the minimum needs of my family?

- Which things, although not considered to be "needs," do I still feel are important to provide my family? What trade-offs am I willing to make in order for my family to have those things?

What's My Salary Really Worth?

The fundamental decision you must make is whether you intend to live within your income. If you decide to do this, you cannot spend more money than you earn. This takes a real commitment.
James Stowers

Although you may be fortunate enough to live off of dividends, interest or money from investments or inheritances, chances are you are one of the many who must trade their time for the money they receive.

While work requires a huge investment of time for most of us, it can also be very rewarding. Many jobs demand lots of creative, productive, problem-solving and social energy. This is a great opportunity to build self-esteem and prove your worth in the marketplace. Work is also a means to an end. Without it, you may not have the financial resources to raise your family and live the life you desire.

 CFP TIP *Love to Work*

One of the best values you can share with your children is the love of work. The easiest way to teach this is by role modeling for your kids a positive attitude about working and your job.

No matter how much money you earn, you may find yourself asking, "Is the trade of my time worth the money I earn?"

Part of living your parenting values is investing your time and money wisely. In order to find the right balance for your family, you need to first figure out what it costs your family in "non-negotiable" expenses. Then compare this to your total income, less the amount you spend to earn your income. In other words, what does your income cost you and what does it buy?

MONEY MATTERS

Depending on where you live and the type of child care you choose, you can spend anywhere from $4,000 to more than $10,000 per child per year. Because younger children usually require more attention, costs for them tend to be greater than for older children.

Money earned is just one factor in answering these questions. You also need to zero in on the things that are important to you, or your values, in your parenting, work and personal life. Remember, not all of your income is used for your family's needs. You also pay a portion of your wages just to keep your job.

Here is a look at some of the costs associated with going to work.

Child Care: The Cost of Putting Your Children in Good Hands

For many families, child care is one of the highest financial tradeoffs associated with working. Some families are lucky enough to have relatives who will watch their kids for free. Other parents pay up to $300 and more per child per week.

Costs can rise during the summer. It all depends on what kind of lessons, summer camp, sports and other activities you want your children to experience.

Transportation: Driving Is No Bargain

Though Carolyn's job is only four miles from her home, by the time she gets to work every morning, she's driven 20 miles. That's because the daycare she loves is eight miles in another direction. Before she even arrives at work, Carolyn spends more than $7 for transportation, gas and maintenance. That's $35 a week and as much as $1,800 a year.

Another Example

Fred takes the train to work. He drives six miles to the train station each morning, buys coffee, a pastry and a newspaper and spends an hour riding to work. His costs include gas, maintenance, parking at the train station, price of the ticket, coffee, pastry and the newspaper – almost $11 a day.

Some families are lucky enough to have relatives who will watch their kids for free.

Clothing and Grooming: The Price of the Professional Look

One of the questions Sandra asked on her job interview was about the company dress code. She was told that the policy was "business" dress. Professional clothes and accessories can be expensive. In addition to the initial cost, many of her clothes required dry cleaning. On top of that, her job required that she look her best every day. That meant frequent manicures and hair styling. All combined, it added more than $100 a month to her costs of working.

Career Eating: Taking a Bite out of Your Salary

If going out to lunch is a regular part of your workday, consider this – even a modest $5 lunch each day will gobble up $25 a week or $1,300 a year. Why not consider bringing a sack lunch from home? A sandwich, chips, fruit and dessert can cost around a dollar. Frozen entrees can be bought for a little more than a dollar.

Parties, Celebrations and Events: The Cost of Being a Jolly Good Co-Worker

Some "days" cost more than others – Secretary's Day, Boss's Day, birthdays, weddings, births, showers and holidays are among the many work-related events and celebrations that will compete for your time and money.

Being part of the community of co-workers is fulfilling, fun and financially demanding. You have to chip in on your boss's anniversary gift. Your co-worker's daughter has finally found a great guy to marry and you have to get her a wedding present. It's your assistant's birthday and that calls for a gift and a special lunch.

While these may represent a small price to pay for being part of the group, the combined expense of these events can quickly add up and needs to be included when you look at what it costs for you to work in your job.

MONEY MATTERS

To save on transportation expenses, consider driving an economical hybrid car, using your community's public transit system, carpooling or riding a bicycle.

Write down your

expenses as

they happen.

Paying Your Dues

Some of the other, less obvious, expenses associated with a job include licenses, continuing education, membership in trade and professional organizations and industry magazine subscriptions. Although your employer might reimburse you for some of these expenses, many companies expect their employees to pay for these things.

What's It Cost?

Try identifying your major work-related expenses by tracking them for a couple of months. This will help you determine exactly how much it costs for you to be employed.

Here are some ways to keep track:

- Write down work-related expenses in a small tablet at the end of every day.

- Write down your expenses as they happen (if you're around other people, this could inspire an interesting conversation).

- Keep your receipts and enter them in a financial tracking software program or make up a log similar to the following example.

	Child Care	Commuting	Clothing/Grooming	Food/Snacks	Dues	Incidentals	**TOTAL**
MONTH:							
DAY 1							
2							
3							
4							
5							
6							
7							
8							

	Child Care	Commuting	Clothing/Grooming	Food/Snacks	Dues	Incidentals	**TOTAL**
9							
10							
11							
12							
13							
14							
15							
16							
17							
18							
19							
20							
21							
22							
23							
24							
25							
26							
27							
28							
29							
30							
31							
TOTAL							

MONEY MATTERS

According to a recent study from the Family and Work Institute, more than half of the employees interviewed said they sometimes felt overworked or overwhelmed. Managers, Baby Boomers and mothers tend to feel more overworked than other employees.

While you're doing this exercise, ask yourself these questions:

- Am I earning enough to justify working, or is my salary simply paying for the opportunity to work?

- If I didn't work, would the family need to replace my salary, or would my time at home offset the loss of income?

- Am I happy with the way I spend my work-related time and money?

- Are there ways to reduce my work expenses and make better use of my money?

- Is my income worth the price I pay in time and energy?

- If I'm not happy with my current work and money situation, what are my options?

Both my husband and I had good jobs and made good incomes. But I felt I didn't have a handle on where our money went. Figuring out the cost of working had a big impact on me. I was able to see just how much of my money was, in a sense, "pre-spent." I figured that if I rearranged my carpooling schedule, and flexed my hours even two days a week, I could save money on after-school care and have more time with my kids. My husband also put in for a flex day. Saving money motivated us, but the real prize was getting in that extra family time.

Deidre, mother of three

When I reviewed my expenses, I was surprised at how high my transportation costs were. I decided to explore ways I could save on gas and parking. That inspired me to put together a rideshare for three days a week, take a bus one day a week and drive my car on Friday, when I needed to pick up the kids and run errands.

Richard, father of two

If you find that the trade-off from working does not balance with the time and commitment you want to make to your family, you might want to consider some of the following options:

- Finding another full-time job that is more flexible and parent-oriented
- Asking for flex-time
- Job sharing
- Telecommuting
- Working part-time
- Starting a home-based business
- Quitting work and living on one income

My employer has been very supportive. In order to make my single income stretch, he told me I could bring my baby to work for the first year. We set up a playpen area in my office and my daughter, Morgan, came with me for more than a year. One of the other assistants was always around to help me and pitch in if Morgan was fretful and I was on a deadline. My boss's flexibility saved me thousands of dollars, hours of stress, and created a wonderful group of supportive adults for my daughter.

Jennie, mother of one.

"We set up a playpen area in my office."

Income Reduction – Living on Less

Before we had children, my wife, Virginia, and I both worked. But we were worried about becoming dependent on a two-income lifestyle, because she wanted to stay home, once we had children. So we decided to live only on my earnings, while saving and investing all of Virginia's salary. This decision proved to be the right one for us. Eventually, when Virginia reduced her hours to part-time so she could spend more time with the kids, we were spared the shock of being forced to drastically reduce our standard of living.

James Stowers

In today's society, many young couples start off marriage with two incomes. In some cases, the second income is a necessity, while in others it is used to increase the couple's standard of living. Sometimes, though, a couple may find themselves in a position where they need to evaluate the possibility of living on a single income.

For some families, having a parent at home is an important value, so they decide to adjust their lifestyle to a single income when they have children. Unlike years past, when it was expected that the mother give up her job to stay home, today's families can use creativity to come up with solutions that work best for them. Of course, some moms still want to stay home; but some couples select the parent with the lowest income to stay home or the parent who has the skills to do it the best. Other couples take turns, one works for a couple of years while the other stays home. Then, they switch places.

MONEY MATTERS

You might also consider the negative costs of staying home. It may be hard for the home-based spouse to re-enter the workforce. This makes the person staying home financially more vulnerable in terms of future earning power and career building.

Other parents find themselves forced into a one-income situation, through down-sizing, company closings, health issues, burn out or other situations.

Without pre-planning, taking the giant step from two incomes to one income may mean a big adjustment. To do this may require a change in lifestyle and a stronger commitment to be financially responsible. You might have to postpone or cancel some of your planned purchases. You need to accept the fact that you can't have everything in life and then make difficult choices about the things you do want.

But, if staying home with your kids is a top priority, you will find ways to make things work out. For starters, before becoming a single income family, draft a new budget and see what life will be like on one income.

Some things to consider:

- What work expenses (such as clothing, transportation and food) will disappear or change when you stop working?

- Will you need to make adjustments for benefits that came with the other income, such as health insurance, life insurance and retirement?

- Are there benefits to being without one of the incomes (like more time to spend with the kids, less stress rushing to accomplish errands or household tasks and more time for community involvement)?

- Do you have expenses at home that you can do without, such as cable TV, high speed Internet or cell phones?

- Are there things that you pay other people to do that you will have time to do yourself (child care, house cleaning, laundry, lawn care, household maintenance)?

- Which expenses are necessary? Are there any less expensive alternatives, such as moving to a smaller home?

Some couples take turns, one works for a couple of years while the other stays home, then they switch places.

After you take a careful look at your budget, you may decide that you still need two incomes. Can you get by without two full-time salaries? For example, you might want to consider looking into flex-time, alternating shifts, a home-based business or other options that allow you to continue earning some income while feeling less rushed and stressed.

Becoming a one-income family is not just a financial decision. Depending on your current lifestyle and the ages of your children, the reduction of expenses can initially have a psychological impact on your family. Here are some tips for anticipating some challenges as you adjust to one income and being a stay-at-home parent:

- Talk to your kids about your decision and how it will impact the entire family, as well as each individual. In addition, talk about what you will need to reduce or give up. Be sure to discuss how this decision will benefit each of you, as a family.

- Be aware of the psychological impact that staying at home can have on an efficient, busy, career person. Your spouse may be relieved or panicked. He or she may feel liberated or trapped. Make sure you talk about these feelings as they come up and develop an understanding as quickly as possible. Relationship issues may also arise. One spouse may expect the at-home person now to do all the housework while the at-home person may still expect the employed partner to help.

- Before and after the change, find other parents who live on one income. Get support and advice from them. Just as you did at work, it's important to build a network of friends who can share this experience with you.

Are there things that you pay other people to do that you will have time to do yourself?

CFP TIP   *Home Alone, Almost*

For many parents, staying home after a fast-paced career can initially be challenging. They may feel isolated and overwhelmed. They are not used to creating their own structure.

"I started taking my daughter for strolls in the parks, just to get out of the house," says one parent. "Then I started talking to other parents who were there with their children. Soon I had a new circle of friends and my life felt richer."

Here are a few other experiences from parents –

Like Minds

Our lifestyle really changed when we decided to live on one income. We started living more simply. Fortunately, my kids were little and barely noticed the change. By the time they got older, we had a group of friends who were all doing the same thing, so they had peers who understood the challenge of living on a single income.

Shirley, mother of three

Clean Clothes Make a Difference

When my kids were little, I wanted to focus on my career. When they got older and were in school, the effects of daycare were impacting all of us – they were tired, and I was burned out. No matter what I did, I couldn't get organized. We only saw the kids a couple of hours in the evening, and those hours were packed with activities. This hectic pace affected our nutrition and our moods. Our lifestyle was not working.

> *"Our lifestyle really changed when we decided to live on one income."*

"Financially, we have

ups and downs."

I quit my job and we jumped into living on one income.

Now, I'm there for my kids before and after school. We eat meals at home much more often. We are more organized. We have clean clothes and the kids have a more consistent bedtime. Those little things have made a big difference.

Financially, we have ups and downs. I used to have lots of anxiety about money even when I was working. Now when that feeling comes over me, I look around at my blessings and how our family life has improved. That helps me stay calm.

Tiffany, mother of two

Practicing One-Income Living

Before our first child was born, we tried to live on one salary and put my salary in the bank. When I got pregnant, we started calculating how much we would save when I stayed home. We would save on:

- Taxes

- Clothing dollars

- Meals out

- Child care

- Gas, maintenance and vehicle wear and tear

We added up those things and it looked like we would have enough, but somehow we ended up on the short end.

Then we thought of other ways to save money and not crimp our lifestyle. I like to cook, so we saved money by eating at home. I had fun figuring out how to live nicely on our reduced income. In the beginning, we had to work at it, but now it seems easy and natural.

Darlene, mother of three

One Plus: Bridging the Earnings Gap

As you've read in earlier chapters, sometimes one salary is not quite enough. Sometimes, the parent who was eager to stay home is not quite fulfilled. When that happens, it's time to explore options for flexible earning.

Consulting, home-based businesses, part-time work and telecommuting are some of the many options. Here's one mom who enjoyed trying different options.

Piecing Together an Income

When my second child was three months old, we discovered our babysitter was not taking good care of our children. I was very upset and quit my job to stay home and care for my kids. I also watched my nieces and nephews.

My husband quit his automotive business, which had taken up much of his time and energy, and began working for a nearby parochial school. I helped at the kid's preschool part-time in exchange for their tuition. I also babysat three days a week for the children of teachers.

Two years ago, the preschool offered me a full-time job teaching. I declined because I could make more money babysitting three days a week than I could working full time.

Many cities have special requirements for home-based businesses. Contact your state, county and local governments and ask about:

- Permits
- Taxes
- Insurance
- Building Requirements

An extra bonus of doing daycare in our home is that we deduct part of our utility bills. This helps offset my earnings so we don't pay as much in taxes.

I don't work during the summer. With four kids, I would be spending more than I was making by sending them to camp. It's like I'm running my own "day camp." I love it.

Sara, mother of four

"...we created a home based business so we could be near our kids."

Exploring Options

About two years ago another stay-at-home friend and I began talking about creating our own business so we could make some money. Both of us wanted to be with our kids and wanted to do something that paid us for our time. We started a catering business that we can expand as our kids grow older.

It's good to look at your strengths and see what you can do – either starting a business or doing contract or part-time work. You have to have confidence in yourself and take a chance. If you're hard working and you have a goal, you can have the best of both worlds ... time with your children and a job that's fulfilling.

Kelly, mother of three

Work as a Hobby

I work on a limited part-time basis and put the money I earn into savings. I know we will need it in the future. My husband has a full-time day job and also has a computer business at home.

At first, I felt he was spending too much time with the computers, especially since his business wasn't making any money. But he explained how this little business relaxes him and gives him pleasure. And even though it's not making money, it does make enough to fund itself. It's like a self-funding hobby.

Susan, mother of two

Getting the right balance between earnings and parenting is a skill that's worth practicing. In our next chapter, we'll show you how to match your values with your spending.

MONEY MATTERS

A home-based business may qualify you to take tax deductions on your mortgage and utilities.

NOTES

_____

_____

_____

_____

_____

You Are What You Buy

Matching Your Values with Your Spending

Home Works

Driving a Good Bargain

Making the Most of Windfalls, Raises and Other Extras

Saving Without Suffering: Tips for Reducing Expenses

Look at your purchases to see if your spending matches your values.

How you spend your money is a reflection of your family's values. How many times have you stopped and analyzed your purchases? How often do you buy something because you want it, not because you need it? This chapter encourages you to look at the decisions behind your spending and shows you how you can save a lot, both financially and emotionally, by spending less. Here are the topics we'll cover:

- **MATCHING YOUR VALUES WITH YOUR SPENDING** helps you decide if you really need to spend top dollar, or if you can find a less expensive way to get the things you need.

- **HOME WORKS** shows you how your housing choices can influence your long-term financial plans.

- **DRIVING A GOOD BARGAIN** offers some new ways to look at transportation.

- **MAKING THE MOST OF WINDFALLS, RAISES AND OTHER EXTRAS** explains how you can make the most of the extra money that comes your way when you have a savings plan.

- **SAVING WITHOUT SUFFERING: TIPS FOR REDUCING EXPENSES** gives quick and easy tips for finding extra money.

"If you have a question about how much you should pay for something, remember it's worth only what someone else is willing to pay for it."

James Stowers

Matching Your Values with Your Spending

Perhaps you've had the experience of watching a brand-new, designer baby frock happily destroyed in one exuberant meal. Or, maybe you've witnessed new toys shattering after only three adventures. You might have seen your child's feet outgrow those expensive name-brand shoes before the shoes show any wear. Given the circumstances, you can't help but think about all the other things you could have done with that money.

I am always looking for good value. When our children wanted to take piano lessons, I knew I didn't want to spend money on a new piano. I called a friend who was in the piano business. He referred me to a piano restorer who found a wonderful used piano.

Stephan, father of two

MONEY MATTERS

To extend the life of your appliances, make sure everyone in the family knows how to operate them properly.

Part of connecting your spending with your values is figuring out when to go for high quality and when to head right for the bargains. Where and when does quality really matter to you in terms of status, aesthetics or how long the item will last? Once you decide you want great quality, how can you get the best possible value and make certain you're getting your money's worth?

Here are a few questions to help you in your decision-making:

- Is this something you need, or is this something you want?
- If it's something you need, what are the alternatives to buying it new? Can you borrow, lease, rent or get this used? Is the cost of any of these options considerably less than if you bought it new?
- If this purchase is something you want, how long have you wanted it? If you wait another week or month, will the desire go away?
- What are you willing to give up to buy this?
- What are the benefits of this purchase? How does this support the family values you want to develop?
- Does this purchase benefit the entire family or just one or two members?
- Are there other, less expensive ways to get the same benefits?
- How long will this item last? How long will the benefits last?

As a family, brainstorm alternatives to the purchase. This isn't intended to make you change your mind, just to expand the way you think about the item you're thinking about buying. You may find that your purchases have more meaning and greater value when the entire family helps make the decision.

Before our daughter was born, we decided to buy a large freezer. We wanted one that would last, so we researched freezers and watched for sales. We bought a high quality freezer at a good price. That freezer was a great purchase for us. It's never needed service and has allowed us to save lots of money by buying groceries in bulk.

Darlene, mother of three

Home Works

We rented for five years. We'd been saving for a down payment on a house, but area housing prices were skyrocketing. We couldn't keep up. Then my husband discovered a special program where municipal employees could buy houses for nothing down. He contacted them to find out if something similar could be set up for state employees (which is what we are). They said, "yes." All it took was one phone call. We bought a modest fixer-upper for nothing down.

Pam, mother of one

The single biggest expense for most families is a home. While many people dream of owning their own home, it's not always the best decision. For some, home ownership is a source of constant stress – taxes, yard work, maintenance, painting and plumbing. For others, home ownership provides a great deal of satisfaction. In spite of the demands, they find owning a home very rewarding.

"A large freezer allowed us to buy groceries in bulk."

If you do buy a home, you want it to be a true shelter and an asset, not a financial and emotional drain. It needs to be affordable and meet the needs of your family. You want to be able to afford it even in the "worst of times."

We started off in an apartment, then moved into a little house. Even though we could afford a bigger home, we didn't need it. We waited to move into our current, larger, house until after our daughters were born.
Ayeesha, mother of two

...decide whether this type of move is in your best financial interest...

Before you consider buying a home or moving to a bigger home, make sure the move brings you closer to your life values and your financial goals. To help you decide whether this type of move is in your best interest, consider your answers to these questions:

- Are you moving because you have to or because you want to?

- Is your current space still large enough for your family?

- If your income was reduced, could you afford your new home?

- What features or benefits will you gain with the new home?

- Is it financially more sensible to remodel your current residence in order to get the features you want?

- How long do you anticipate you'll live in your new residence?

- Do you have the time to maintain it yourself or will you have to hire someone to do the upkeep?

- Are there any additional costs (e.g., property tax, utilities, maintenance) associated with moving to a new home?

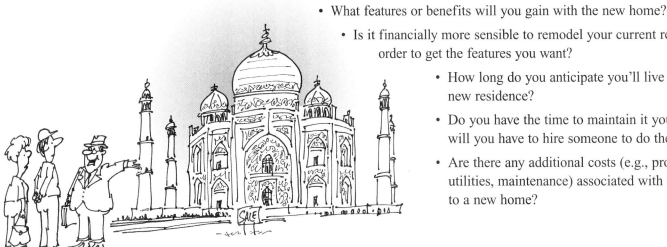

Sometimes, people move into a certain type of home or a higher status neighborhood to support their career.

For example, Fred and his family decided to move to a larger house in a high-status neighborhood. Both he and his wife worked. Their careers required them to do a lot of entertaining and networking. With that in mind, they analyzed the move and decided that the new house, which was perfect for gatherings and meetings, would be a good investment.

Even though a luxury home was not on the family's list of priorities, the move gave them an opportunity to advance in their careers and increase their income. This allowed them to do the things that were really important to them like saving for college and a comfortable retirement.

Here's another "moving" story.

Last year all of our friends either built or moved to bigger and newer houses. I was surprised at how that affected me. I felt like a failure. Our friends could afford nicer houses, why couldn't we? I felt depressed and dissatisfied with our house and myself. Finally, my husband said, "If you really want to move, we can. Here's what we need to do." He laid out the amount of money it would take and what we would have to give up. When I looked at it that way, I realized moving wasn't in the best interest of our family. A big house isn't as important to me as some of our other priorities. I'm grateful my husband reminded me of that. Without the added expense of a bigger home, we can continue to save for our kids' college, plan for retirement and enjoy traveling.

Susan, mother of two

MONEY MATTERS

Stay on top of changing interest rates. When rates are low, consider refinancing your home to get a more favorable rate. By reducing your rate by one percent, you can save thousands of dollars or trim several years off your mortgage.

CFP TIP *Home Sweet Planning*

Some parents have a specific plan for when they want to make housing changes. They plan how long they will stay in their first house and often plan to stay in their second home until the kids are grown.

Driving a Good Bargain

We never borrowed money to buy a car. During the early years of our marriage, when all our friends were driving nicer and newer cars, we thought many times about selling some of our investments to buy a new car. But our desire to be financially independent was stronger than our desire to keep up with others. We kept driving our sturdy old car, which worked perfectly well.

James Stowers

Having children can change your idea of transportation.

Having children can change your idea of transportation. Before becoming a parent, you may have imagined yourself behind the wheel of a jazzy little sports car. Now, you cringe at the idea of trying to cram a car seat (or two) into the tiny back seat of a two-door car. With kids, your idea of great transportation could be a boxy looking minivan, with room to easily buckle in your three kids while carrying all their stuff and the groceries.

Everyone has his or her own idea of the perfect car. For some, it's style and performance. For others, it's safety and reliability.

Whatever you think the ideal car looks like, consider how the car you drive supports your values and goals. Before you jump into the driver's seat of a new set of wheels, consider these questions:

- Will your car just be used for commuting to and from work, or will it also serve other purposes?

- What are the most important characteristics you look for in a car?

  Gas mileage

  Safety

  Style

  Reliability

  Status

- Can you buy the kind of car you think you need without going into debt?

- Can you buy an older model of the same car for less and still get what you want?

- How much is the insurance? How much is the personal property tax?

Beware of hidden costs. Cars are a good example. The price of the car is just the beginning. Then you have insurance, personal property taxes, licenses, maintenance, gas and repairs.

Can you buy the car you need without going into debt?

I look for the best value in a vehicle. I don't steer away from a car just because it's got 80,000 miles on it. I take it to a great mechanic and have it checked out. I save thousands because I don't mind driving an old car.

Stephen, father of two

We started our marriage with two cars and ended up selling one of them. With the money we saved by not having that second car payment, we were able to make the down payment to buy our first house.

Ayeesha, mother of two

You can actually save money by closely following your car's maintenance schedule. That way, small problems can be found while they're still small and less expensive to fix.

When we moved to a house near a bus line, I started riding the bus to work. We still had two cars, but I wanted to save parking expenses and the hassle of the drive. After our first child was born, our expenses grew. We decided to sell one of the cars to offset the additional cost of our child. Even though it created a slight inconvenience, the trade-off was worth it.

Jared, father of two

Making the Most of Windfalls, Raises and Other Extras

Your boss calls you into her office.

"I've been meaning to talk to you about your work," she says. You feel your throat tighten. "Your work has been outstanding lately, and I want to give you a bonus to show my appreciation."

You can barely contain your delight. The rest of the day, all you can think about are ways to spend the bonus – a family vacation, a new suit, or perhaps you'll splurge and get the new bedroom suite you've been wanting.

Then you get home and your spouse reminds you, "We agreed to save at least half of any extra money that comes our way."

You are disappointed and glad at the same time. Investing part of that extra money in your family's goals is one way to really zoom ahead financially.

We have a strict rule that we save all extra money that comes our way. It's so tempting to want to spend it right away. But we know how secure we feel when we boost our savings.

Ralph, father of two

We treat windfall money like it's income. We donate a percentage of it, save a percentage of it in our long-term savings and put the balance in short-term savings to fund our family activities.

Arnelle, mother of one

 CFP TIP   *Raising the Savings*

Some people have a plan to save or invest any "new" money. So, whenever they get a raise or bonus, they immediately know what they're going to do with it.

What is your plan for using and or saving extra or unexpected money? If you don't have a plan, take some time and figure out what's best for you and your family. By focusing on your values and goals, you may be able to find a way to make your long-term dreams a reality.

Saving Without Suffering: Tips for Reducing Expenses

A secret to financial success is to live below your means. We've tried to adhere to that. Sometimes people look at us and ask, "Shouldn't you be driving a better car or living in a better home?" I ask, "Why?"

Stephen, father of two

MONEY MATTERS

If you're buying a car, you will save a lot in interest if you can delay making the purchase until you have enough cash. However, if you can't wait and need to borrow money, check with your bank or credit union. They may be able to offer a lower rate than the car dealer.

Imagine a faucet that slowly drips all day. The drips are small, yet you know that over time they add up to gallons of water.

Now imagine your own spending drips, little leaks in your economy that don't really benefit you and your family. What could you do with those "gallons" of money? How can you save more money without giving up the things you enjoy? For most people, that is an on-going question. Everyone has his or her own techniques for curtailing spending. The things you choose need to make sense for your family. Here are a few ideas from other families.

Food Stuffs

You can save money if you get into the kitchen and cook from scratch. We eat a lot of veggies and we eat no meat at home. We all help prepare meals – it not only saves us money, but it's also great family time and teaches the boys domestic skills.

Jodi, mother of three

You can save a lot of money using coupons and going to discount stores. I never go to the grocery store unless I have $30 in coupons. I make it fun – it's a game for me. I love to shop with coupons. I get a real feeling of accomplishment seeing how much money I save.

Sara, mother of four

Fix those financial drips.

I plan a menu every week and buy only the ingredients I need. I stay away from prepared foods because they cost more per serving.

Pam, mother of one

We joined a wholesale club, and buy bulk food that I know we'll use. To make certain I don't impulsively buy things we won't use, I always have a list and stick to it. I also get the kids involved with coupons. When we go shopping, the kids take the coupons and find those items in the store. Once in a while, I'll add up the value of the coupons and give that amount to the kids as a reward.

Darlene, mother of three

My husband creates a menu and does the grocery shopping. He's a better shopper and spends less than I do.

Gwen, mother of one

I used to buy my lunch at work practically every day. I was surprised at how much I was spending. So, now, two days a week, I take a can of soup. My lunch expense went from as much as $7 a meal to around $1.50.

Stephen, father of two

We have three kids. When we eat out, it can be very expensive. By going to restaurants that let kids eat free, we can feed the entire family for A LOT less.

Keyla, mother of three

MONEY MATTERS

*According to the **Consumer Price Index**, telephone services account for more than 2 percent of consumer spending.*

Communications and Entertainment

Every once in a while, we talk about getting cable TV. We have looked at how much cable costs vs. the cost of renting videos or borrowing entertainment from the library. We don't have enough time to sit in front of the TV for the hours it would take to justify the expense of cable.

Jodi, mother of three

When we first got cable TV, we signed up for a lot of the premium channels. We soon realized we simply weren't watching them. We got rid of the extra channels and cut our cable bill in half.

Even though a subscription to the daily newspaper is expensive, we found a way for it to pay for itself. Every week we look at the ads, coupons and entertainment section listing family-friendly free activities. We end up saving enough money to pay for the subscription and even come out ahead.

Sara, mother of four

We have reduced our long-distance costs to nothing by using our cell phone for long distance.

Our parents, who live out of town, don't have cell phones so we give them phone cards as gifts. That benefits us both. They can call at no expense, and we can talk more often.

Darlene, mother of three

"By going to restaurants that let kids eat free, we can feed the entire family for a lot less."

CFP TIP   *Call Them On the Bill*

Examine your phone bills at least twice a year. Look at your calling habits and see if there are ways to reduce your expenses.

Utilities

We save money by using a setback thermostat. At night when we go to sleep and during the day when we're not home, it adjusts the thermostat to use less energy.

By using water-saver showerheads, we not only save money but I get hot water after my daughter has been in the shower. So it's also a self-preservation tool.

Finally, we buy energy-saving light bulbs. They are a little more expensive, but we end up saving enough on our electricity bill to make up the difference.

Ayeesha, mother of two

Checklist for Savings

Are you doing everything you can to reduce your expenses? Here is a sampling of some areas where you may be able to cut back and find extra money to invest:

- Adopt a cash-only policy – it's mentally harder to spend cash than it is to use a credit card.
- Cancel your cable or satellite TV subscription.
- Eliminate the "premium" movie channels.
- Cancel magazine subscriptions.

"We save money by using water-saver showerheads."

- Have only one telephone line.

- Use a free dial-up Internet service provider instead of paying a subscription fee.

- Find a lower cost long-distance provider (free long distance is part of many cell phone rate plans) or consider using a calling card. It may take a little longer to place your call because you have to dial more numbers, but the savings can be significant.

- Limit the amount your family spends on gifts.

- Find a way to turn a hobby into money (for example – sewing, photography or painting).

- Get books from the library rather than buying them at the bookstore.

- Visit a local playground instead of going to a restaurant play area.

- Sell your second car and live with only one, or use the money to buy a lower priced used car and invest the difference.

- Always, ALWAYS pay your bills before they are due to avoid late charges and interest fees.

- Depending on the season, adjust your thermostat up or down so you use less energy. You can also use a setback thermostat to adjust the temperature automatically throughout the day.

  - Do one full load of laundry instead of several small loads.

  - Wait until the dishwasher is full before you run it.

  - Buy shampoo, and other liquid soaps, by the gallon. Then, pour it into smaller bottles.

  - Maintain your car so it's running at peak performance.

Cancel your health club membership if you're not using it.

- Turn off lights, TVs, radios and other electronics if you're not using them.

- Cancel your health club membership if you're not using it.

- Eat more meals at home.

- Cancel your cell phone subscription.

- Have a garage sale or auction items online.

- Use a water-saver showerhead.

- Clip coupons, but only for things that you normally buy.

- Use energy-efficient light bulbs.

 CFP TIP   *The Value-Added Homes Tour*

What does cost have to do with the things you really love?

Take your family on a tour of your house. Start in your favorite room. Rate your furniture from one to three, three being the chair everyone wants to sit in and one being the fancy wooden antique even the dog doesn't like. Notice if the top scoring pieces are also the most expensive.

Continue the tour in your children's room. Ask them to rate their top ten items.

End up in your closet, where you evaluate your favorite clothing. This is a fun exercise to do when you're feeling like you don't have enough money to do what you want to do. You may also learn that the things you're fondest of are not the "best" or most expensive.

This is also a great way to get ready for a garage sale. Those low-rated "ones" could make room for something you'd enjoy more.

Debt Defying Ideas

Debtor's Chains: How We Get Into Debt

Ten Proven Ideas to Avoid Credit Card Debt

Staying Out of Debt

Debt can come from financial emergencies such as having to replace a roof …

I f you have credit card debt, you are not alone. One survey estimated that the average American household has at least one credit card and owes more than $8,000 on it. If that sounds like you, can you afford to continue falling deeper into credit card debt? This chapter gives you ways to understand what causes debt and shows you how to pay off your credit cards. On the following pages, you'll read about:

- **DEBTOR'S CHAINS: HOW WE GET INTO DEBT. It starts out harmlessly enough but can escalate until you're overwhelmed with stress. Here are some of the ways you get into debt and some of the stress it can cause you.**

- **TEN PROVEN IDEAS TO AVOID CREDIT CARD DEBT provides you some easy and practical ways to get out of the plastic trap.**

- **STAYING OUT OF DEBT. Celebrate National Cut-Up-Your-Credit-Card Day™ by making a commitment to live free of all credit card debt.**

Debtor's Chains: How We Get Into Debt

You work hard at what you do, but at times the kids can push you to your wit's end. It's natural to feel as though you deserve a break. You deserve to get out and have fun. You deserve to go out to eat at that fancy new restaurant or to buy something new.

But you also want to live a balanced life that is relatively free from financial pressures and stresses. To make this happen means getting out, and staying out, of debt.

Many of us have been in a situation where we used a credit card (or two) to help us squeeze through a month filled with financial obligations or emergencies. These can include:

- Loss of income due to job loss, salary reduction or having to take time away from work for family or health reasons.

MONEY MATTERS

The average American household has six bank credit cards, eight retail credit cards and two debit cards.

- Financial emergencies such as unexpectedly having to replace a roof, furnace or car.

- Family members who need emergency financial help.

- Dance lessons, school fees, clothing or other expenses for your children.

Debt can also come with major purchases, such as a home, car or educational expenses. For some, these types of debt are a natural part of life, but they don't have to be.

Is your anxiety over debt affecting your behavior at home?

When we got married, we had $35,000 in debt from school and car loans. Our first goal, before we had kids or bought a house, was to pay off that debt. During that time, we didn't go out much or spend much money on unnecessary things. Our only major purchase was a computer, so my husband wouldn't have to go into the office on the weekends. Within two years we paid off the debt and we had money to put down on a house.

Susan, mother of two

What Happens When You Get into Debt?

Being in debt can have a psychological, as well as a financial, impact. Worrying about financial issues rates high on the stress scale. Some people feel a heaviness settle upon them. They feel depressed. They experience sleeplessness, a sense of futility and shortness of temper. They feel hopeless and out of control.

If you're worried about debt, you might be cranky with your children. They will know something is wrong, but they won't know what.

CFP TIP   *Spill the Beans, Ease Your Worries*

If your anxiety over debt is affecting your behavior at home, sit down and talk to your children. Apologize for being short-tempered and assure them your moodiness has nothing to do with them and that they are still safe and cared for. If your children are teenagers, you may want to share with them the source of your concern. Ask them if they have any suggestions for ways the family can help reduce spending. Children sometimes have amazing insights and suggestions in these areas.

Adopt a cash only policy.

Ten Proven Ideas to Avoid Credit Card Debt

Who would have imagined the power you could wield or the havoc you could wreak with a slim rectangular piece of plastic? Who would have guessed the terrible grip that innocent-looking plastic card could get on your mind and your life?

Breaking yourself of credit card dependency and emerging from debt is an empowering experience. When you are free from debt, you feel lighter, more hopeful and better able to live out your dreams. These tips give you some easy ways to make your debt-free dream come true.

Tip 1. Pay with Cash Only

For many people, walking out the door without their credit cards is a strange and unsettling experience. They feel a vague sense of uneasiness. What if there's an emergency? What if they need something right away? What will they do?

Leaving your credit cards at home is a great first step to getting rid of credit card debt. Now you no longer have an instant way to borrow money.

When you adopt a cash-only policy, you have to pay attention to what you are buying. You can't randomly purchase extra items.

Larger ticket items also require greater planning and consideration. You can use this extra time to your advantage. Ask yourself several questions. Including:

- Do I really need this item? How will it benefit me and the family?

- Are there alternative ways to get this item or the benefits it offers? Borrowing, leasing, substituting?

- What other costs (such as maintenance, upkeep, fuel, etc.) come with this item?

- Is the quality of this product equal to the amount of money it costs?

- What else could I buy with this money?

Do I really need this item?

The first time I left my credit cards at home and went shopping, I felt strangely vulnerable. I was walking into a discount department store armed only with my list and cash! I didn't have a back-up system. I realized I was going to have to stick to my list and pay attention to the prices. The stress soon gave way to a feeling of concentration and accomplishment. I walked out of the store with exactly what I needed and nothing more. When I had my credit card, I might easily have added an extra $50 worth of impulse purchases.

Dee, mother of two

Tip 2. Understand the Difference Between Needs and Wants

If we want to buy something we don't really need, we wait one hour for every $10 of the purchase price. Most of the time, the desire to have whatever we wanted goes away.

David, father of two

CFP TIP   *Delay Gratification*

When you have a burning desire to buy something, and you feel it's your right as an adult to buy what you want - take a break. Write down what you want. Wait a week or so. See if it's still important to you.

One of the keys to freeing yourself from debt is to understand the difference between what you and your family need and what you want. Most of us have wants that seem like needs. The desire to have a new car or washer/dryer can be so strong, you wonder how you will ever get along with what you currently have. But, think back now to the values and priorities you established in Chapter Two. Do your wants match what you have established as your priorities? If not, it should be easy to stick to your needs.

 CFP TIP   *A Child's Mind*

While a favorite stuffed animal may seem like a want to an adult, to a child this could be a very strong need. In order to feel safe and secure, children like to surround themselves with certain things that help define who they are ... for some it may be a stuffed animal. For others, it's a toy, pillow or blanket. When you discuss wants and needs with your kids, keep in mind their needs may not reflect what adults think is practical.

In order to feel safe and secure, children like to surround themselves with certain things that help define who they are ...

Separating your wants from your needs may require effort and discipline. This could leave you feeling deprived or depressed. To avoid these feelings, be creative about finding new, less expensive ways to get what you want. For example:

Want a new outfit? See if you and a friend can trade an outfit or two. That way you get to wear something new, without paying anything.

Think that a few sessions with a personal trainer will transform your life? See if you can find a trainer who will barter with you, or gather a few friends with your same training needs and share the costs.

Feel like you will scream if you have to keep sitting on that ugly old sofa? Try garage sales, estate sales and thrift stores for something used. Or ask your friends if they know any people who are moving and have furniture to give away or sell cheap.

After twice running our credit card debt up to large amounts, we decided not to buy any unnecessary items until the cards were paid off. We try not to use our credit cards at all anymore. It's a lot easier to do than we thought it would be.

Pam, mother of one

Tip 3. Corral Your Card

Every time you use your credit card or borrow money, you are committing part of your future earnings. If you spend more than you earn, you are "mortgaging" your future.

James Stowers

We've all seen images of wild horses, bucking and running free across an open prairie. Unfortunately, some people act the same way with their credit cards – spending freely and with reckless abandon.

Unlike the horses, when it comes to debt, we need to establish boundaries and not exhaust our resources by spending wildly.

A credit card can be extremely convenient, but there are times when a cash-only policy might work best. Begin by analyzing your credit card bill. Study it and look for:

- Purchases under $20

- Impulse items, such as candy, gum, magazines, soft drinks

- Fast food or restaurant meals

- Movie and video game rentals

Do you really want to pay 18% interest (or more) on a pack of gum? When you start limiting your credit card usage you can begin to rein in your debt.

Tip 4. Negotiate a Lower Interest Rate

If your household is like most, every other day the mail brings you a tantalizing offer from a credit card company.

If you want a lower interest rate without the hassle of changing credit cards, you will be amazed at what a simple phone call to your credit card customer service department can do for you. In a recent survey, more than 50% of the customers who called and asked for a lower rate, got one. Some customers lowered their rate five points or more. If you're going to pay interest on your credit card purchases, which would you rather pay 18% or 13%?

If you decide to change to a credit card that charges a lower rate, be sure to read the fine print. Some low-interest rate offers last only a couple of months, then balloon to higher rates.

Call your credit card company and tell them you want a lower rate.

CFP TIP   *Pay More and Save*

Even if you get a lower rate, continue making the same payment. You'll pay off your debt faster.

Tip 5. Put Your Savings to Work

When you're trying to pay down your credit card debt, look for and take advantage of any opportunity to save money. If you're not clipping coupons, start. Sign up for a "rewards" card if your grocery store offers it. Make sure to mail in rebates and cash-back offers.

Then, add up the money you saved and include that extra amount on the check you send on time with your credit card payment.

 CFP TIP   *Take It From Savings*

If you have savings or investment accounts that are earning a lower rate of interest than your credit card charges, why not consider using those savings to pay off all your credit cards? It will save you money in the long run.

Tip 6. Debt Consolidation

Practically every bank now has some kind of "debt consolidation" loan. This lets you take out a short-term loan, using your house or car as collateral and then use the money to pay off your credit card. The bank loan should be at a significantly lower interest rate than your credit card. When you pay off your credit card, vow never to get into that type of debt again.

If you decide to change to a credit card that charges a lower rate, be sure to read the fine print.

If you pay off your credit card with a debt consolidation loan, you may be tempted to go shopping to celebrate. Fight that impulse! Just because your credit card balance is zero, you're still not debt-free. You still have to pay off the bank loan. Consider paying this off quickly by making extra payments or by making payments equal to the interest rate you were paying on your credit card.

James Stowers

 CFP TIP   *The Bigger They Are ...*

If you owe on more than one credit card, pay off the card with the highest interest rate first.

We prefer to take money out of savings to pay off our credit card bill rather than carry a balance. If we want to buy a big-ticket item, we save until we can afford it. That way we pay cash for it. One trick we found is that some places will give a discount when we pay with cash. With cash, the store doesn't have any processing fees to pay to a bank or credit card company.

Darlene, mother of three

Tip 7. Seeing Time as Money

Before you buy something with your credit card, think about what it costs in terms of hours, not dollars. If you want to go out to a nice dinner, think about how many hours of work the meal will cost you. Is it worth it? Are there better ways to spend the money you earn … especially when you think about the time and energy it takes to earn it? What else can you do with the money you save by eating at home?

Seeing time as money.

Show your children how to look at their "must-haves" in terms of hours, as well. How many hours will it take for them to earn money for their latest want? This is a great way to start putting time and money into perspective.

Tip 8. Just Say "No Owe"

Have fun practicing the art of consumer resistance. Go shopping and take no money or credit cards. Decide in advance that you are not going to buy anything, you are only going to look.

Pick out an item you want. Think about it as you stroll the store, noticing other things you'd like as well. Do you still want the first item, or is something else more interesting now?

Often times, within the same store, you can find several things that you want to have. Start prioritizing these wants and pay attention to how things move up and down your list. This is a great way to notice your shifting priorities. By simply window shopping you can satisfy your desire to see new things without spending money.

It seems as though you always want something you can't afford. As newlyweds, our entertainment was walking and window shopping. One winter day we walked by an exclusive fur store. We stopped and admired one of the beautiful fur coats. I asked my wife, Virginia, if she wanted it. She said she really did, and then added, "but we can't afford it because it would reduce our investment savings." We continued on our walk. A year or so later, after we had saved some money, we happened to walk by the same store again. We stopped to look at the beautiful coats. I asked if she wanted one of them. This time Virginia didn't answer me right away. Finally, she said, "No, I don't want one." I asked why. She said, "If I had one, I would lose the earnings on the

---

MONEY MATTERS

One survey shows that almost 80 percent of people with credit cards do not pay off their full balance due each month.

money it would take to buy the coat. Also, I would have to pay for insurance and storage. No, I would rather have my money working for me."

James Stowers

 CFP TIP   *Catalog Shopping*

This is a great activity to do with your children, especially during the holiday season. To see how quickly people's wants and priorities can change, look through a gift catalog with the idea that you're just looking and not really going to buy anything. Agree that each of you can select one item from the catalog. Anytime you want something new, you have to give up the last thing you selected. Count the number of times you and your kids change your mind.

Pay your bills before they are due.

Tip 9. Pay on Time

Do you know that some credit cards require your payment to be in by a certain time on a certain day? If you're late, they can then charge you a late fee. Some are as high as $35. To avoid the fee, you must pay your bill before it is due.

Next time you get your credit card statement, read the fine print on the back. This will tell you when your payment needs to be received and how soon after you buy something you will begin to be charged interest. Some cards have extremely short turnaround times. If you are uncertain as to when these dates are, call the credit card company and ask them. Typically, the grace period ranges from seven to 21 days.

MONEY MATTERS

Some banks will allow you to have your bills electronically deducted from your checking account every month. If the fee they charge is less than what you'd spend on postage to mail the bills, this may be worth considering. It also helps make certain your bills are paid before they are due.

In addition to avoiding late fees and interest charges, by paying on time you also:

- **Keep your credit history clean.** Constant late payments will show up on your credit report and make it more difficult for you to borrow money.

- **May be rewarded with a lower interest rate.** Many credit card companies will raise your interest rate if you have a history of late payments. By paying on time, you reduce the chance of that happening.

Tip 10. Pay Yourself First ®

Invest in your future before you spend for the present. On a regular basis, before you pay your bills, put aside a certain percentage of your salary to save for your future. By building your cash reserves, you put yourself in a position to adopt a cash-only policy and free yourself from the credit card trap. For more information about this strategy, see page 199.

Staying Out of Debt

The holidays put enormous pressure on people to buy. Unless you prioritize your spending, you can easily fall into the credit card trap and over-extend yourself financially.

James Stowers

Once you are out of debt, pay attention to how you use your credit cards. Use them only as a convenience, not to fund a lifestyle you can't afford.

Also, mark October 16th on your calendar. This is National Cut-Up-Your-Credit-Card Day.™ On this day, think about how you are spending money and the impact your credit card habits have on your long-term financial success. Try not to spend money on anything you don't absolutely need. If you do buy something, pay cash for it. Have a family conversation about money to review your values and priorities.

> *We got rid of all but one of our credit cards. That was big. We got rid of eight credit cards. By using only one card we have a better understanding of how we're spending our money and manage it much better.*
>
> Sara, mother of four

The holidays put enormous pressure on people to spend more than they earn.

The Long-Term Commitment to Saving and Investing

Time can be your best friend.

It's much easier to spend money than it is to save it. Saving money for the long-term requires discipline and determination. It means you need to fight the temptation to satisfy all your wants and desires. To improve your financial position, get into the habit of saving more than you spend.

This chapter will give you some of the essential facts about money. It's important to understand these because they will help you achieve your financial goals. Included in this chapter is information about:

- **THE SHRINKING DOLLAR shows how money, left alone, will eventually lose value over time.**

- **THE JOY OF COMPOUNDING explains how, when time and rate of return work together, you can take advantage of compounding.**

- **TO THE BANK gives you some things to consider before putting your money in a bank.**

- **UPPING THE INTEREST LEVEL: MONEY MARKETS, CDS AND OTHER SAVINGS INSTRUMENTS offers alternatives to a regular savings account.**

- **INVESTMENT BASICS gives you tips for finding investments that are right for you.**

- **THE STOCK MARKET provides the essential facts necessary to understand common stocks.**

- **MUTUAL FUNDS OFFER A DIVERSE INVESTMENT discusses mutual fund investing.**

- **INVESTMENT ATTRIBUTES CHART compares the attributes of various savings and investment options.**

Before we can begin any discussion on saving and investing, it's important to understand a very *important concept* - **the shrinking value of a dollar**.

"When my wife and I were first married, we agreed that we would never borrow money to buy anything but our home. If you go through life thinking that money is a disposable and infinitely replaceable resource, you are destined to fall short of financial independence."

James Stowers

The Shrinking Dollar

We've all heard stories of how in the 1900s, you could have purchased dinner for four in a fancy restaurant, left a generous tip and received change – all from a single dollar bill. In the mid 1970s, you may remember going to your local fast food hamburger franchise and buying a burger, fries and drink for less than a dollar. Today, for the same dollar, you can buy only the hamburger (provided you have some extra change for tax).

On average, the dollar has continuously lost value. In fact, if you had a dollar in 1900 and just held on to it until today, its buying power would be worth less than five cents.

The only way to be certain your money tomorrow will be worth what it is today, is for it to be in a savings or investment vehicle that is earning an annual rate of return greater than the rate the dollar is shrinking. If you leave $10 in your wallet, a week, a month or a year from now, that $10 may only buy $9 worth of goods or services.

If you held on to a 1900 dollar until today, it would be worth less than five cents.

The Joy of Compounding

It is essential to start saving and investing regularly and early in life.

James Stowers

As the CFP, you should understand the concept of how to make money with money. This is known as **compounding**.

To help explain the concept of compounding, let's turn to Mother Nature for a quick lesson. A farmer can plant a **single seed** of wheat, care for it and from it create more than 100 seeds. If these 100 seeds were planted and properly cared for again, they would produce at least **10,000 more seeds of wheat**. This is the concept of compounding – money, properly cared for over time, will grow and multiply.

The amount of money you can accumulate through compounding depends on two critical factors: **time** and the **annual rate of return**. Time is the most fundamental. The longer you let your money work, the greater your chances for long-term financial success. By putting your money into investments that achieve a higher rate of return, the less money you must set aside.

To illustrate the magic of compounding, take a look at the following chart:

Compound Results of a One-Time Investment of $100
Compounded Monthly

	10 Years	20 Years	30 Years	40 Years
At 6% interest	$182	$ 331	$ 602	$ 1,096
At 8% interest	$222	$ 493	$1,094	$ 2,427
At 10% interest	$271	$ 733	$1,984	$ 5,370
At 12% interest	$330	$1,089	$3,595	$11,865

Money, properly cared for over time, will grow and multiply.

This chart shows you how a one-time investment of $100 would grow over time at various interest rates. As you can see, at an average annual interest rate of 12%, $100 would grow to $11,865 in 40 years.

The following chart shows what happens when you make a one-time investment of $100 and then make a commitment to add $10 each month.

Compound Results of a One-Time Investment of $100 + $10 Monthly
Compounded Monthly

	10 Years	20 Years	30 Years	40 Years
At 6% interest	$1,821	$ 4,951	$10,647	$ 21,011
At 8% interest	$2,051	$ 6,383	$15,997	$ 37,337
At 10% interest	$2,319	$ 8,327	$24,589	$ 68,611
At 12% interest	$2,630	$10,982	$38,545	$129,513

Earning 12% interest, at the end of 40 years, you would have $129,513. Your total investment would be only $4,900 ($100 initial investment + $4,800 ($10/month for 480 months)).

The Four Keys to Accumulating Wealth

1. *Start investing as early as possible. It takes significantly less money to accomplish what you want when you have more time working for you.*

2. *Save on a regular basis. It is an easy way to accumulate wealth.*

3. *Begin investing with the largest possible sum. You will have more money working for you over a longer period of time.*

4. *Reach for the highest rate of return that's safe for you. Each additional percentage point is important. The higher the rate, the less money it takes to accomplish what you want.*

James Stowers, from *Yes, You Can ... Achieve Financial Independence*

To the Bank

A savings account can make you more thoughtful and less impulsive about your spending. If you want your money, it requires a trip to the bank. You can't just open up your wallet or write a check when you dash out to the store.

A savings account at a bank also has these advantages:

- Your money can earn a modest interest.

- It's guaranteed safe by the Federal Deposit Insurance Corporation (FDIC) up to $100,000.

When you put your money into a savings account, you are actually **lending money** to the bank.

MONEY MATTERS

The Rule of 72:

To find out when your investment will double in value, simply divide the number 72 by the rate of return your investment receives. For example, if an investment is receiving an 8% return, it will double in value in 9 years (72 ÷ 8 = 9). The higher the rate of return, the quicker the investment will double.

Savings accounts, Certificates of Deposit (CDs) and bonds are actually **loans** you give to a bank or institution. In return, you are paid a fixed sum of money (interest). At the end of the loan period, or upon demand, the full amount you lent is returned to you.

The Bank Choice

Here are some things for you to consider before selecting a bank. Ask them:

- Is there a minimum amount required to open a savings account? Some banks have a minimum balance amount. This can range from as little as $1.00 to more than $1,000, depending on the bank. Choose a bank you can afford.

- Is there a monthly fee if you don't maintain a certain balance?

- Is the account federally insured by the FDIC?

- What are the best interest rates? Are the rates compounded, meaning, is interest paid both on the principal and accumulated interest?

Savings accounts, Certificates of Deposit and bonds are actually loans you give to a bank or institution.

Upping the Interest Level: Money Markets, CDs and Other Savings Instruments

Although a savings account is an easy, safe place for you to keep your money, an account's interest rate may not be equal to or exceed the rate a dollar is losing value. There are other options which may offer higher interest rates. They include:

- Certificates of Deposit (CDs)

- Money Market accounts

- Bonds

Taking Note of CDs

As we mentioned before, when you "buy" a CD you're really not buying anything, but lending money to the bank for a set period of time. In return, the bank will pay you a set interest amount and then return your entire loan at the end of the period. Most CDs require a minimum deposit.

Many banks will reward you with a higher interest rate if you agree to lend your money for a longer period of time. Because interest rates vary, you should shop around to find the best deal. Also, keep in mind there is a financial penalty (or fine) if you ask the bank for your money back before the end of the time period.

Shopping for Money Markets

If you want to look for a higher interest rate than what a savings account pays, but don't want the time commitment of a CD, a money market account could be your next step. Money markets are like a savings account. However, they:

- May pay a slightly higher interest rate (the amount will vary depending on the market)

- May limit the number of withdrawals you can make during a month

- May offer limited check-writing privileges

- May require a minimum investment in the account, with the possibility of service fees if funds dip below that amount

With a U.S. Savings Bond, you are loaning your money to the government.

Bonds

With a bond, you are **"lending"** your money to a company or government entity with the promise of getting it back, with interest, after a set period of time. You may already have United States Savings Bonds, or have given them as gifts. This is really a loan to the government.

Bonds are issued when a government or corporation wants to raise money to do things. For example, a government might issue bonds to help refinance existing debts, build schools, repair a highway or pursue special projects. A corporation might issue bonds to buy another company, expand their current operation or to buy equipment.

Bonds vary according to:

- **Safety** – Bonds rated AAA (as rated by the Standard & Poor's rating system) are at the high end of the rating scale. The rating measures the bond seller's ability to repay the loan. Keep in mind, if the seller has financial problems, it may not be able to pay interest or return your original investment.

- **Type of institution issuing the bond** – Ranging from private companies to government entities.

- **Length of time** you are willing to lend the money. Short-term bonds mature within five years, while long-term bonds mature in more than ten.

Investment Basics

Savings accounts, CDs, money market accounts and bonds are relatively "safe" places to keep money ... for short periods of time. However, because they are tied to a dollar, they may not appreciate in value faster than the decline in the value of a dollar. That means, after 10 years or so, you may actually be losing money rather than holding value or making money.

The Investing Decision

Earlier in this chapter, we talked about "lender" investments – savings accounts, CDs, money market accounts and bonds. Now it's time to up the ante and look at "owner" investments. Through owner investments, you have the opportunity to become an owner in property, common stocks and mutual funds.

There are two big differences between **lender** and owner investments. The first is risk. As an **owner**, you willingly assume a greater degree of risk than when you are a lender. The second is **rate of return**. Because you are willing to take a greater risk, you also have the opportunity to realize a greater rate of return.

"There is no such thing as a perfectly safe investment, free from all risk."

James Stowers

It's important to take a minute now to understand the word **risk**. Whether you are a lender or an owner, you assume some risk. Smart people do not seek to avoid risks, but simply try to hold them within reasonable limits. What's reasonable for you and your family may be different from what's reasonable for another family. We all have different levels of risk we're willing to accept.

If you keep your money in lender investments, you risk losing its value over time. There are advantages to being an owner. An owner receives **all** the profits. There is no ceiling on the income or financial gains you may enjoy (compared with the fixed interest offered by savings accounts, CDs, money market accounts and bonds). But the biggest advantage is that owner investments are free from the dollar's shrinking value.

Along with the advantages of ownership comes risk. The risks of owner investments include:

- Owners absorb any losses incurred by the investment.

- There are no guarantees of a return on your investment.

- Profits are generally unpredictable.

- There is no guarantee of the value you will receive for the property if you choose to sell.

We all have different levels of risk we're willing to accept.

> *The best time to plant an oak tree was 20 years ago. The second best time is today.*
>
> James Stowers

Patience is key when investing. Time can be your best friend. If you get off to an early start, it generally takes less money to reach your financial goal (whether it be a college education, early retirement or financial independence) because your money will be at work for a longer period of time. Time also allows you to overcome errors in judgment along the way.

Investments can earn money the following ways:

- **Appreciation** – They can increase in value over time such as baseball cards, stocks or real estate.

- **Dividends** – Income received as an owner of a business.

- **Capital Gains** – Profits received from the sale of assets.

At the end of this chapter is a chart that compares the characteristics of the different ways you can save and invest. To help you better understand these concepts, take a couple of minutes now to review this chart.

The Stock Market

Ownership of a **publicly owned corporation** is divided into "shares" of what is called common stock. Each share represents a fraction of the total ownership. The term "common" is by no means negative; all owners of a corporation are **common stockholders**.

Not every corporation is willing to share its ownership. Some companies are **privately held** and don't sell shares to the public. The easiest way to distinguish between private and public companies is to look at the stock tables in the newspaper. Only those companies that are publicly traded will be included in the stock tables.

If you were to trade your dollars for common stocks, you would have the most to gain from a successful business and the most to lose from an unsuccessful one. Common stocks in **successful companies** may come closer to offering all the advantages of an ideal investment than any other financial medium.

A good place to start understanding how common stocks work is the daily newspaper. Look for articles in the financial section and national and international news about public companies.

A good place to start understanding stocks is the daily newspaper.

Stock Picks

Two options are available to you if you want to invest in common stocks. You can either blindly accept what others tell you, or you can take time to study and understand the essential facts that can affect you. Only when you understand the facts can you develop confidence in what you believe and why you believe it.

Let's be blunt. Blindly accepting what others tell you can be a foolish path to follow. You need to understand the essential facts regarding the characteristics, the short-term risks and the long-term opportunities of owning common stocks. For some, buying common stocks can be like gambling. If you don't know the facts, you have about as much chance of succeeding in the stock market as you do in a casino.

Review the chart at the end of this chapter to understand how common stocks compare to other investments. Keep in mind, this chart is not all-inclusive. There are many factors you should consider before you invest.

Making smart investment decisions requires an enormous amount of research and the resources to analyze the data. That's why so many people are now turning to professionals to help them manage their investments.

Blindly accepting what others tell you can be a foolish path to follow.

The Dow Jones Industrial Average

To help you grasp the stock market's ups and downs, it might be helpful to understand the Dow Jones Industrial Average (often referred to as **"the Dow"**). The Dow is the oldest and most widely quoted stock market gauge. Experts believe it represents the overall market at any moment in time.

The Dow is made up of a selected group of 30 stocks. These stocks are chosen by The Wall Street Journal.

Look at the following graph. It shows the history of the Dow (accurate data is available as far back as 1896).

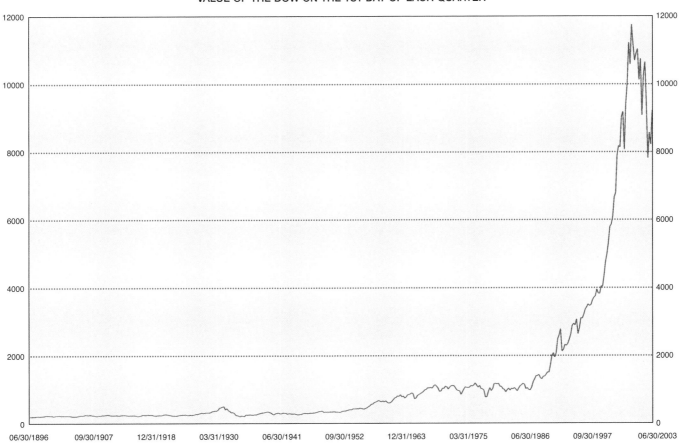

VALUE OF THE DOW ON THE 1ST DAY OF EACH QUARTER

Here are some things to consider as you review the graph on the previous page:

- **Fluctuations** – The value of the Dow goes up and down like a roller coaster. Most changes are minimal, but occasionally (like in the 1990s) they are dramatic.

- **Long-Term Upward Trend** – The long-term trend of the Dow has been up since 1896.

- **Spurts (Uneven Trends)** – The upward trends are uneven. Many of the major moves are in spurts, few of which were predicted.

- **Always Rising to New Highs** – Since 1896, the Dow has always risen to new highs over time.

Information about the Dow can be found in the business sections of most major newspapers and on the Internet (look at cnnmoney.com or usatoday.com). If you haven't invested in stocks before, tracking the Dow can help give you confidence in the potential of the stock market, as well as provide a continued understanding of how it operates.

Mutual Funds Offer a Diverse Investment

I believe the soundest and safest place for me to invest my own money is in mutual funds that are searching for and investing in companies that are successful with earnings and revenues that are growing at an accelerated rate.

James Stowers

Mutual fund investing allows you to put your investment choices into the hands of professional managers. A mutual fund is a collection of stocks or stocks and bonds put together for a specific goal, such as growth or income. When you buy mutual funds, you are actually purchasing small amounts of many different stocks and/or bonds. Compared to other investments, mutual funds offer many benefits. These include:

- **Professional Management** – Mutual fund managers are full-time professionals dedicated to managing the money invested in their funds. They bring with them a specialized team of researchers, analysts and technological tools to make certain that the money invested, no matter what the amount, is given full-time attention. They invest, reinvest and seek the best opportunities for the money they manage.

- **Diversification** – Unlike buying shares of individual stocks, mutual funds spread investments over a number of different companies and sometimes industries. Diversification is beneficial since some companies may lose value while others prosper. This means the losses of one company can be offset by the gains of another.

- **Opportunity for Growth** – If the past is any indication, common stock mutual funds offer an opportunity for growth, particularly over the long term.

Professional management uses the latest technological tools to invest your money.

- **Available in Convenient Amounts** – Many investment options require a large initial investment, which closes the door to the small investor. Some mutual funds offer investment plans that allow investors to begin with a modest amount and add additional amounts on a regular basis.

- **Liquidity** – Depending on the strategy of the fund, you may be able to withdraw part or all of your investment at any time. Some funds may require that you wait a period of time before you get your money to discourage you from "playing the market" and over-reacting to market fluctuations.

- **Current Information** – Information about your mutual fund investment is readily available. Simply call your mutual fund company or visit their Web site to track your account's progress.

It is important you understand the investment philosophy of the mutual fund you intend to invest in.

How to Choose a Fund

There are literally thousands and thousands of different mutual funds.

In theory, all mutual funds have access to the entire common stock and fixed-income market, but not all are solid performers over time. How they differ depends on the combination of investment objectives, performance, ethics, qualifications of the managers, dedication and available support systems.

It is important that you understand and believe in the investment philosophy, objectives and policies of any mutual fund in which you invest.

To determine if a fund matches your personal values, consider how you would answer the following questions:

- Is the fund's philosophy logical? Does it make sense?
- How does the fund intend to implement its investment philosophy?
- Does it follow its discipline consistently year after year, or does it change its approach frequently?

    Most importantly, examine the investment results of the fund.

- What is the record of the investment manager?
- Has the fund been successful over time?
- Are the results consistent?
- How do the results compare with those funds that have similar objectives?

Of course, the fact that a fund, or any investment for that matter, performed well in the past does not necessarily mean it will in the future.

 CFP TIP *Steady as She Goes*

Regular investing can enhance your potential for making a reasonable profit over time. When share prices vary, investments made at regular intervals may reduce the average cost of a share. Therefore, your investments may ultimately outperform a one-time investment.

> ## MONEY MATTERS
>
> *"One of the advantages of owner investments is they are free from the shrinking value of a dollar. Time erodes the value of a dollar but enhances the value of owner investments."*
>
> James Stowers

Investment Attributes Chart

Use the table below to compare the attributes of various savings and investment options. This chart is divided into two categories, Lender Investments and Owner Investments.

	LENDER INVESTMENTS					OWNER INVESTMENTS					
	Savings Account	CDs	Money Market	Savings Bonds	Piggy Bank	Collectibles	Gold	A House	Individual Stocks	Stock Mutual Funds	Fixed Income Mutual Funds
Is there a minimum amount of money required to get started?	Maybe	Yes	Yes	Yes	No	No	Yes	Yes	Yes	Yes	Yes
Can you get your initial money back?	Yes	Yes	Yes	Yes	Yes	Maybe	Maybe	Maybe	Maybe	Maybe	Maybe
Is your money easy to withdraw?	Yes	No	Yes	No	Yes	No	Maybe	Maybe	Yes	Yes	Yes
Is it burglar proof?	No	Yes	Yes	Yes	No	No	Maybe	No	Yes	Yes	Yes
Can your money grow faster than the shrinking value of a dollar?											
Short-Term*	Maybe	Maybe	Maybe	Maybe	No	Maybe	Maybe	Maybe	Maybe	Maybe	Maybe
Long-Term*	No	No	No	No	No	Maybe	Yes+	Maybe	Yes+	Yes+	No
Can your money benefit from compounding?	Yes	No	Yes	No	No	No	No	No	No	Yes	Maybe
Is your money professionally managed?	Yes	Yes	Yes	Yes	No	No	No	No	No	Yes	Yes
Will you get regular progress reports?	Yes	Yes	Yes	Yes	No	No	No	No	Yes	Yes	Yes

* Short-term investments are less than five years. Long-term investments are those greater than five years.

+ Historically, these investments have grown faster than the shrinking value of a dollar. However, past performance is not an indication of future results.

NOTES

Emergency Money Reserves: A Solid Strategy for Surprising Times

The Attack of the Unexpected

Create Your Emergency Fund

Build Your Own Fort Knox

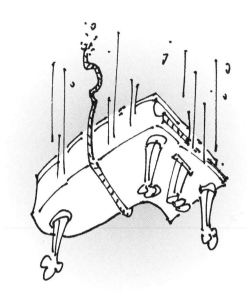

The attack of the unexpected.

Many of us have plans that have gone in directions opposite of where we thought they'd go – from having the value of an investment portfolio fall, to having job raises vanish, to suddenly being laid off.

Perhaps you've read the book, ***Alexander and the Terrible, Horrible, No Good, Very Bad Day***, by Judith Viorst. We've all had days like Alexander experienced, where almost nothing goes right. Perhaps it starts with the dog eating one of your brand new expensive running shoes. Then you discover, for the second time this month, a puddle of water in the den. You realize either you get the roof fixed soon, or you'll need a small boat to get across the den. Then your freezer gets a hot flash and more than half of your food, which you saved lots of money on because you bought in bulk, is ruined. Those are just the little things. We haven't even mentioned the big stuff, like medical conditions you never knew existed and job loss.

So how do you protect yourself from such outrageous misfortunes? This chapter helps you financially prepare for the unexpected.

- **THE ATTACK OF THE UNEXPECTED introduces you to just a few of the things that can suddenly go wrong and explains why you should have an emergency fund.**

- **CREATE YOUR EMERGENCY FUND gives you a simple three-step plan that shows you how to create a financial security blanket.**

- **BUILD YOUR OWN FORT KNOX shares the tips and experiences of other parents who have created their own safety net.**

Sometimes we go in the opposite direction of where we planned.

The Attack of the Unexpected

If you don't provide for your emergencies, who will?

James Stowers

These days it's easy to anticipate that you'll encounter the "unexpected."

- Carolyn went to work as usual. At 10:00 she went into her scheduled performance review meeting with the CEO of the small company she worked for. At 11:00 she was reeling from shock at her boss's words: "You're a great worker. We hate to let you go. But things are tough, and we have to drastically downsize your department."

- Evan was an only child, with a child of his own. When his mother broke her hip, he thought she would spend a couple weeks in the hospital and then return to her own home. But his mom experienced complications. Her hospital stay was extended. Finally, her doctor recommended she go to an assisted living facility, rather than back home. Unfortunately, his mom didn't have the money for assisted living. So, she turned to her son, Evan. He was the only one who could help.

- Two days after the warranty on Betty's refrigerator expired, something happened to the motor. The repair person came out, looked it over, and said, "It will cost you more to fix this than it will to buy a new unit."

These are just a few of the unexpected things that can happen to us. It's hard enough dealing with daily emotional stress, but worrying over whether you can make it through the next month heightens the tension considerably. That's where your emergency financial reserve comes in.

Create Your Emergency Fund

During the early years of our marriage, we figured that, if monthly expenses were $2,000 a month, six months emergency reserve would be $12,000. That's a lot of money to be invested at a low interest rate. We felt we could not afford to do this.

Instead, we hurriedly accumulated the $12,000 in a growth fund as the foundation of our long-term plan. Then we kept saving for the future. By doing this, we always had money we could use as collateral from which to borrow money for emergencies and we kept our long-term plan growing.

We were still able to do everything we truly wanted to do during our life and educated all of our kids. Now we can do what we want, when we want.

James Stowers

How would you handle a financial emergency?

What would you do if a financial emergency struck? Where would you get the money to live? How much money should you have?

Here's a three-step plan that will help you get started.

1. Determine How Much You Need

Decide how much you want in your emergency fund. Many experts advise three to six months of living expenses in reserve. Even if you have far less, a small reserve can still increase your peace of mind and give you a feeling of financial flexibility.

The first step in developing an emergency fund is determining your typical monthly expenses. List your fixed expenses, such as your mortgage or rent, car payment, utilities and other payments that you make on a regular basis. Then list your variable expenses such as entertainment, personal care, vacations and other costs that you don't have on a regular schedule.

As you review your expenses, consider whether all of them are necessary. For example, can you trim your expenses by reducing your entertainment options or eliminating club memberships and magazine subscriptions? Eliminating things you've gotten used to may be difficult to do, but when you're using your emergency funds to pay for them, it may be necessary.

Here are some expenses to consider when determining the size of your emergency fund. Remember, you're planning for three to six months of expenses.

MONEY MATTERS

Not everyone can save enough for three to six months expenses. If this is not realistic for you, look for other solutions. Can you borrow against a CD, investments or use your home as collateral? Can you establish a home equity line of credit for emergencies?

Taxes	federal and state income taxes, real estate taxes, personal property taxes
Real Estate	mortgage or rent payments, insurance, maintenance, second-home costs
Utilities	electric, gas, water, trash, phone, cable/satellite/Internet
Vehicles	loan or lease payments, insurance, personal property taxes, license, maintenance, gasoline
Health Care	medical insurance, out-of-pocket costs, prescriptions, glasses or contacts, dental
Personal Care	toiletries, cosmetics, hair care
Food	groceries
Clothing	new clothes, laundry soap, dry cleaning, tailoring
Vacations	travel, lodging, food, entertainment, souvenirs
Entertainment	restaurants, tickets, movie rentals, books, CDs
Savings/Contributions	education or retirement savings, contributions to charities
Memberships	health club, social club, professional organization
Student Loans	loan payments for tuition and related educational costs
Miscellaneous	gifts, magazines, newspapers

The amount of money in your emergency fund may vary, but it should be large enough to prevent you from selling your investments – possibly during unfavorable market conditions – to pay for emergencies.

2. Figure Out How to Save Consistently

Decide how you will go about saving this money. A payroll deduction is a great way to save for emergencies. Even $25 from each paycheck adds up. Or, review the budget you created in Chapter Three and look for areas where you can trim expenses. Deposit the money you save into your emergency fund.

Once your emergency account reaches the desired balance, monitor it and make any adjustments based on your current financial needs. As time progresses, you may need to increase the amount in your account in order to maintain your current lifestyle.

3. Find a Safe Place to Put Your Savings

Figure out where you will put these emergency savings. You want an account that is:

- Readily available

- Safe, with the return of your money guaranteed

- Income-producing

You might consider an interest-bearing checking or savings account through a bank, credit union or savings and loan. You might also consider a money market account.

Some families divide their reserves. They keep the first three months of reserve money liquid and they go to short-term CDs for the second three months. That way, they earn slightly higher interest and can borrow against the CD if need be.

 CFP TIP   *Study Up on Severance*

When you are considering how much emergency reserve you need, consider your severance package, if you have one. How long does your health insurance coverage last? What type of severance pay can you expect? What other benefits are you currently getting that you could lose if you lost your job?

Does your company offer a severence package?

Build Your Own Fort Knox

When Melanie's position got downsized, she took her severance package and put it in savings. That was the beginning of her emergency fund. After she got another job and times were good, she was frequently tempted to use that money on a trip to Europe with the children, a new car or a remodeled kitchen. But she always found other ways to make those dreams happen. Ten years later, when she was downsized again, she had a comfortable emergency reserve to get her through the months of job searching.

Without emergency funds, you might have to dip into or borrow against retirement funds or other investments. You might have to pay penalties. You might need to take out a second mortgage or home equity loan. Creating an emergency fund takes discipline, but the peace of mind and the flexibility you gain make it worth the effort.

Here's are some ways other parents manage their emergency fund:

Save Your Emergency Money Through Payroll Deductions

We use payroll deductions to make direct deposits into our emergency reserve. It's a small amount every month, and we really don't miss it. Because it goes directly into our savings account, we're not tempted to spend it.

Darlene, mother of three

Build your own financial fortress.

Put All Found Money in Your Emergency Account

The balance of our savings account is several thousand dollars. We're able to keep it growing by putting money directly into the account from our paychecks. We also put any money we receive as gifts into the account.

Pam, mother of one

Find Ways to Pay Back Your Emergency Account

When it came time to replace our roof, we dipped into our emergency fund. We knew we could quickly replace the money we were taking out, because that same month, we were paying off our car loan. Once that was paid, we continued to make monthly payments, except this time it was to ourselves. It took about two years, but our emergency fund is again fully funded.

David, father of two

Teaching Preparedness

Unexpectedly, we had to buy a car this year. Our emergency savings paid off – we bought the car without taking out a loan. We used this occasion to talk to our daughters about the importance of this kind of emergency savings.

Susan, mother of two

MONEY MATTERS

If you get into an emergency that forces you to take out a home equity loan, shop around for the best bargain. Beyond the interest rate, some banks require appraisals and other costs are involved. Find out the total cost before you choose your lender.

A Closer Look

Family Start-Up Costs

Market-Proof Your Kids

Gift Giving That Works for You

Learn as They Earn: The Value of Work

Pay Yourself First®

Educate Yourself On College Plans and Savings

Life Insurance

Spending Time Without Spending Lots of Money

Affording to raise a family isn't just about money.

Maintaining your priorities while raising your family can be very rewarding. One of the keys to staying balanced and focused on your goals is to have the kind of information that helps you make smart decisions.

This section gives you additional details on some of the topics concerned parents frequently ask about. These chapters are designed to be short and precisely focused on a single topic. On the following pages, you'll read about:

- **FAMILY START-UP COSTS helps you control the initial expenses you can expect during your child's early life.**

- **MARKET-PROOF YOUR KIDS shows you how to teach your children to protect themselves against relentless advertising.**

- **GIFT GIVING THAT WORKS FOR YOU provides tips for giving birthday parties and buying birthday gifts that won't cause you to work overtime.**

- **LEARN AS THEY EARN: THE VALUE OF WORK explains the benefits and how-to's of encouraging your children to work for their extras, from making money at home to branching out into the workplace.**

- **PAY YOURSELF FIRST® describes a sure-fire way to help make your long-term financial dreams come true.**

- **EDUCATE YOURSELF ON COLLEGE PLANS AND SAVINGS offers a quick course on the many ways you can save and pay for your child's education.**

- **LIFE INSURANCE gives you everything you need to know about life insurance in "terms" you can easily understand.**

Finally, we end this book with more than 70 fun and inexpensive ways you and your family can enjoy spending time together. As you know, "affording" to raise a family isn't just about money … it's also about time, energy and attention. As your family's CFP, your kids expect, and need, you to guide and nurture them. In the last section, we'll show you how you can do that by:

- **SPENDING TIME WITHOUT SPENDING LOTS OF MONEY helps you enjoy playing, exploring and learning with your family on a limited budget.**

A Closer Look

Family Start-Up Costs

*Advertisements make you think you have to spend a lot
to provide the best for your baby.*

According to a USDA survey, during your baby's first year you can expect to spend about $10,000 on the things you need to support this new life. If you're not careful, your start-up costs can quickly throw your budget into turmoil.

Your costs for these first expenses will depend on:

- How many of the "extras" you want
- Your shopping expertise
- Hand-me-down possibilities

In addition to these factors, one of the strongest forces working against your budget is advertising. As expectant parents, you will be the target of clever advertisements designed to make you think you have to spend a lot to provide the best for your baby. Although the latest gadgets are attractive and convenient, a baby's needs are really quite basic.

The following list provides you with a sensible starting point for your shopping.

"I was surprised by how much we spent during our baby's first year. Formula, diapers, furniture and accessories are so expensive."

Sara, mother of four

Baby Clothes

As much fun as it is to dress-up your baby in pretty little clothes, remember that for comfort and usability, the clothes best suited to a baby's needs are T-shirts and sleepers.

If a neighbor or relative has a child older than yours, see if you can borrow, or buy, their hand-me-downs. Some groups and neighborhoods have even formed used clothing exchanges where sharing is encouraged.

Food

Breast milk is the least costly way to feed a baby and is highly recommended by pediatricians. However, if you opt to use formula, you will save money by using either the powdered or concentrated formula rather than paying a premium price for formula that is premixed.

CFP TIP   *Sign Up Now*

Many formula makers will send you coupons for their brand. To get your coupons, sign up to be on their mailing list. Look for sign-up cards at your doctor's office or the formula maker's Web site.

Once your baby is ready for solid food, pediatricians usually suggest sticking to basic foods such as plain cereals, vegetables and fruits until about the seventh month. When your baby is ready for combination foods, you can save money by preparing your own foods using a blender or food processor. You can find recipes on the Internet or through your local library.

Buy diapers in bulk.

Crib

One way to save on a crib is to look for a used one, shop at garage sales, or check with a neighbor or relative to see if you can borrow a hand-me-down. Be aware that most cribs made before 1986 do not meet current safety standards. Before you accept a new or used crib:

- Check to see that the frame is solid, with all the hardware and screws.

- Make sure the sides lock firmly into place.

- Check the mattress for firmness. It should fit tightly against all four sides of the crib.

- Make certain the slats are no more than 2 3/8" apart.

Diapers

Cloth is by far the least expensive and most environmentally friendly way to diaper your child. However, if you choose to use the more convenient disposable diapers, you can still save over retail by using coupons and buying in bulk (or, should we say - BULK!). Ask your friends and relatives to help out by clipping coupons for you.

Stroller

Strollers come in many shapes, sizes and designs. What's right for you depends on your lifestyle. Do you live an active life with lots of exercise? There are specialized strollers for when you jog or for pulling behind a bicycle. Some strollers even come with a built-in car seat so your sleeping child can go right from the car into the stroller without waking up. The more features you get, the more expensive the stroller. However, by buying a quality, feature-rich stroller, you may actually spend less than you would buying several items separately.

Car Seat

Research car seats and find the one with the highest safety rating. **This is one area where you don't want to compromise quality for value**. Although more economical, a used car seat may be missing parts or the instruction booklet. This can make it difficult or even impossible to install and use the seat properly.

High Chair

There are many different types of high chairs on the market. Some of them can even be converted to a booster chair or a play chair, although these may cost more.

When shopping for a high chair, you should look for these features:

- A wide base for stability

- A system for restraining your child

- A tray that's easy to remove with one hand and that has a deep rim to contain spills

Disposable diapers can be more convenient.

CFP TIP *They Grow So fast*

While a $70 pair of name-brand sneakers might be cute, your child will outgrow them very quickly. Shop sensibly and save.

As soon as you "know," you can start shopping for roomier clothes.

Much of your baby shopping will be done before the baby is born. During this time, the mother-to-be will also have her own shopping needs. Outside of medical costs, the single biggest expense for a new mom is clothing.

Dressing Up Mom

Maternity clothes can go from bargain basement to designer deluxe. One mom we know never bought any new maternity clothing. Instead, she requested donations from neighbors and sisters. Another mom spent more than $1,000 for a high-class executive wardrobe to keep her looking good on the job. It all depends on what kind of clothes you need, whether you have hand-me-downs and where you like to shop.

When shopping for clothes, keep in mind that mom's body will change often and quickly. Don't buy more clothes than you realistically need for any trimester.

 **CFP TIP** *Outfitting Yourself*

As soon as you know you're pregnant, you can start shopping for roomier clothes. Anticipate the seasons and buy clothing to match your new figure. For example, if you're newly pregnant in October, you may still be able to buy last summer's close-outs. These could be perfect for your third trimester.

NOTES

A Closer Look

Market-Proof Your Kids

Market-proof your kids.

Y̶ou can turn off the television. You can turn off the Internet. You can steer away from the shopping malls. But you can't protect your children from the sophisticated, persistent, consumer-oriented bombardment of advertising. Every day your children are targets. Thousands of marketers aim right at your kids, and their aim often hits the mark. Before your children turn five years old, they have seen and heard at least 30,000 advertisements. These ads are aimed at turning your vulnerable, impressionable, curious children into insatiable consumers.

As consumers, your children are part of a growing market that directly influences $188 billion and indirectly influences $300 billion more of parental spending. Children contribute $25 billion of their own money to the mix. That's why it's important that you talk to your kids and prepare them to be smart consumers.

You are Surrounded, but You Don't Have to Surrender

Your children are bombarded with advertising messages wherever they go. The media feeds them full of brand name wants and desires.

As a CFP, you need to define the place these things have in their lives. Some parents want their kids to have a certain type of clothes and gadgets so they can fit in. Other parents want their children to have only simple things. Other parents encourage their children to earn money for designer clothes and fad items that are beyond the price they want to pay.

How do you share your values about material goods with your kids? How can you give your children the tools they need to be informed consumers?

"One of our biggest concerns is how to raise a child who understands the worth of things and values simplicity."

Here are some tips:

Be a Good Role Model

In spite of the fact that you are largely outnumbered by the media bombardment, you are a powerful role model for your children. Your kids watch what you do and see how you live out your values.

During the next couple of weeks, notice your own consumer habits. Do they reflect the values you want to pass on to your children? If not, start now to change the way you spend your money. Tell your family what you're doing so they can encourage you and participate.

Address the Ads

Talk to your kids about advertising. Show them how marketers will use tricks to make their product more appealing. Watch TV with your children and discuss the commercials you see. Talk to your kids about how advertisements are designed to turn a want into a need. You can do this in the car, too. Look at billboards and talk about what you see.

Another idea is to keep an "ad journal" for a couple of days and write down all the different types of advertising you and your kids notice. You'll quickly realize that ads are everywhere – on the side of a bus, inside buildings and in magazines, just to name a few places. Talk about what you see and hear.

These kinds of conversations make your children more aware of advertising and help prepare them to analyze and deal with its effects.

Your children are watching to see

how you live out your values.

Turn off the Television

Many experts agree that TV commercials fuel the desire to buy. Here are some things parents have done to monitor TV viewing:

- Have certain times when kids are allowed to watch TV.

- Substitute appropriate, commercial free, videos for television.

- Designate certain days as "no TV" days. Be sure to schedule other family activities during that time. The more fun and interesting those activities are, the less attractive television will be.

We never watched TV when our kids were little. We didn't want them exposed to commercials. This policy had great benefits – when holidays and birthdays came around, they never had a long list of stuff they had to have.

Tiffany, mother of two

Write down all the different types of advertising you and your kids notice.

Establish a System for Responding to Buying Fever

Consistency is a great trait. Sometimes we are too tired, worn out and distracted to think through each burning desire our kids suddenly come up with. Before you go into a store with your kids, discuss and agree upon why you're there and what you intend to buy. After you go through this process a couple of times, it becomes easier.

One way to approach this conversation is by presenting your child with one of the following options:

- Yes, you're buying something for your children within a spending range.

- Yes, you're buying them something, but only what is already on your shopping list.

- No, you're buying exactly what is on the list and that does not include anything for them.

- No, you're not buying anything extra, but your kids can if they have the money.

Consumerism has been a difficult issue for us. Our daughter used to scream when she wanted us to buy her something and we said, "No." Now when we go shopping, we make a list of what we're buying and we stick to the list. We explain this to her before we leave. When she asks for something, we tell her, "It's not on the list."

Pam, mother of one

Don't Cave In

"It's not on the list."

Kids will be kids, and no matter how much you talk to them about curbing their wants, your children will want things. They will plead, pester, nag and create some very convincing arguments. They will wear you down with their desires. They will evoke guilt with their rationale. Experts advise, stay firm and don't cave in. If you are consistent in how you treat your kids' requests, they will eventually understand the values you're trying to instill in them.

One of our daughters wanted expensive batting lessons to help her with her softball game. We told her we'd pay for the lessons if she made a commitment to practice. It didn't take long before she stopped practicing. Even though we wanted her to continue taking the lessons and excel at her game, we had to be true to our word and so we quit paying. We told her if the lessons really mattered to her, she would have been more committed to practicing.

Judy, mother of two

The Pressure to Have it All is Intense

The following statistics are based on the results of a national telephone study of 746 American children ages 9-14. The poll was commissioned by the Center for a New American Dream and conducted by Widmeyer Communications.

The results of the poll indicate that the pressure to "have it all" is intense.

- 63% of the children surveyed expressed concern that there is too much advertising.

- 58% feel pressure to buy stuff in order to fit in.

- 74% worry that advertising aimed at getting kids to buy things causes conflict between kids and parents.

- 74% say it's unfortunate you to have to buy certain things in order to be "cool."

- 81% complain that lots of kids place way too much importance on buying things.

58% feel pressure to buy stuff in order to fit in.

A Closer Look

Gift Giving That Works for You

Your generosity can cause you to overextend your budget.

Throughout the year there are ample opportunities to shower your kids and family with gifts. Birthdays, anniversaries, holidays, graduations and other milestone events call for a celebration! Then there's the competitive nature of kids and birthday parties … each trying to one-up the other by doing something bigger or fancier than the last party.

You may enjoy providing gifts or throwing parties, however, your generosity can also create the opportunity for you to overextend your budget. This can leave you feeling stressed and financially strapped.

In this chapter, we'll show you how you can do blow-out celebrations without blowing out your budget.

Party Invitations – The Price of Popularity

You may experience mixed emotions every time your child brings home another party invitation. You're thrilled your child is included and has friends; but as more and more invitations roll in, you begin to wonder, "How can I afford to buy all those presents?"

As a CFP, you may have already included family gifts for birthdays or holidays in your budget. It might also be wise to have a plan in place to cover gifts for those unexpected invitations. Some options to consider are whether you will fund the purchase of party gifts for your children's friends, or if your child will be expected to fund presents from an allowance. Wherever the money comes from, many families find it helpful to set a pre-determined budget for gifts, for example, $10 per gift per friend.

After the gift budget is determined, discuss it with your children. If possible, take them with you when shopping for their friends. They can even be responsible for choosing the gift for the guest of honor, as long

You're thrilled your child is included…

as they remain within the limits of the pre-determined budget. Show them how to compare products and prices. This will not only help your children think about the needs and personality of their friends, but can also be a great lesson for them in becoming savvy consumers.

 CFP TIP   *Consumer Gift-Givers*

Want to train savvy consumers? Take your kids when you shop for their friends' birthday presents. As they consider potential gifts, discuss these questions:

- *Is the gift something the recipient will use?*

- *What other, less expensive, gift options might we consider?*

- *Is it a gift that will be enjoyed for a long time?*

- *What is the quality of the item? Will it break easily?*

> *What other, less expensive, gift options might we consider?*

Big Events on Small Budgets

When it's time for your own child's birthday party, you will probably want to do something original that provides everyone with a fun, fascinating and memorable experience. But what if you can't afford the lavish types of parties all the other children seem to have?

You can accomplish your goal without giving away the farm (or perhaps in your case, the backyard) and all that's in it by following these easy steps:

- Give clear and consistent limits appropriate for your child's age. As a rule of thumb, invite the number of guests that matches the age of your child. By limiting the number of guests, it will not only be easier to manage the party, but will also allow the guests to more easily interact.

Some parents opt to pay for a big party only once every couple of years. Other years, they celebrate less extravagantly by letting their child invite a friend for a sleep over. Some parents avoid big parties altogether, or they team up with a parent whose child has a similar birth date and share the expenses.

Our children went to a small school. If you didn't invite everyone in their class, some children felt left out. We solved the big birthday expense problem by sharing parties with two other girls who had September birthdays. The moms worked together to create a fun party that felt extravagant but was inexpensive because we were splitting the expenses. Plus, it took the pressure off each birthday child and allowed for a more relaxed gathering.

Melanie, mother of two

- Invite your children to help you plan the party. They will love the sense of responsibility they get from being included in the planning. Of course, they won't be able to plan all the details, so your structure and guidance will still be needed.

Older children can also gain valuable knowledge about creating a meaningful and fun party by working with you on the budget. Talk to your kids about how much money you have to spend on the party. Ask:

- What is important to you about this party?

- How do you want to use the money – refreshments, decorations, entertainment or favors?

- Find other like-minded parents and agree on ways to cut down on the extravagance.

Some parents opt to pay for a big party only once every couple of years.

Discuss:

- Limiting dollar amounts on gifts

- Having a gift exchange, where everyone brings something they already have and like but are ready to give away

- Encouraging the giving of hand-made gifts

- Using recycled gift wrap instead of new

Then brainstorm for other ways to have great parties with less pressure.

- Turn your parties into non-gift oriented gatherings.

Have a gift exchange where everyone brings something they already have and like but are ready to give up.

Some parents give parties where the birthday children get to share with others. For example, each guest brings a small amount of money. The money is combined, then donated to a local charity of the child's choosing. Other families have children bring books that are then donated to the library.

Part of the party celebration includes going down to the charity or library and having the birthday child present the organization with the donation. This helps build the children's awareness of "giving" and makes them feel very important.

One of our best birthday parties was also the simplest. We had lots of dress up clothes, including hats, tiaras, old skirts, dresses and costume jewelry. We put it all in a big trunk and let the girls dump it out and dress up. We had easy wash-off make up which they could also apply. They had a wonderful time and the party cost almost nothing.

Clara, mother of three

CFP TIP   *Fun Parties on a Dime*

Children enjoy activities in which they can actively participate. Here are some tips for creative, inexpensive, fun parties:

- *Make papier mâché masks*
- *Create a circus theme – tell fortunes, encourage tricks, act like different circus animals*
- *Make greeting cards*
- *String beads or make jewelry*
- *Have a scavenger hunt*
- *Have a talent show and create a home movie of the performances*
- *Make and decorate cookies*
- *Have a tea party*
- *Celebrate outside - visit a local park or playground*

Create a circus theme...

The Gift of Staying out of Debt During the Holidays

During the holiday season, you want to experience a sense of generosity and compassion toward all. However, if your good intentions get out of hand and you overspend, it can take the fun out of giving.

Here are some tips for staying debt-free during the holiday season and other gift-giving occasions.

Save Year Round

An old-fashioned Christmas Club Account or monthly savings plans are still good ways to save throughout the year for your holiday gift-giving. Every month set aside a certain amount of money in a separate savings or investment account that you intend to use for holiday gifts.

Deck the Halls, with Holiday Goals and Budgets

Before you are swept into the gift-giving frenzy, think about your goals.

Budget everything – including decorations and other holiday extras, then stick to it. The better you plan, the less likely you are to get caught up in the "more is better" cycle.

If your budget is especially tight, talk to your children. Work together on your holiday spending goals and budget. That way, you won't be tempted to promise lavish gifts you can't afford.

If you can't afford gifts for your usual assortment of family and friends, simply tell them in advance. Offer some alternatives – having a cookie exchange, exchanging things you already own, giving group gifts, or each donating a little money and giving a gift to charity.

"We quit holiday gift-giving. Each year, one of us picks a charity and we donate to it. Our children are starting to learn how lucky they are and how wonderful it is to share our blessings."

I lost my job right before the holidays, leaving me with no money to spare. I called my family and friends and told them I could not buy gifts for them – I could only give my children presents. They were lovely and understanding. Once I got over the "shame" of not having enough money, I began really enjoying the holiday season. The stress was gone. The children and I made cookies for some of our favorite people. I felt relaxed and at ease. Even now that I have enough money, I have not returned to my earlier frenzy of getting everyone a present. I honor people by donating in their name to different charities. I have small dinner parties and share the gift of bringing people together. I have learned to enjoy giving, in my own small way.

Melanie, mother of two

Shopping early can help you feel relaxed and at ease.

The Shopping Scheme

We all know those amazing people who shop early and are sipping cocoa and reading home decorating magazines in the hectic weeks before the holiday season. By being organized, they are also being thrifty and wise. They minimize the year-end financial impact of gift giving by spreading their holiday purchases throughout the year.

Try shopping year round. That way, you can take advantage of sales, coupons and special deals as they occur.

Before you go out into the frenzy of merchandise, consider what you'd like to get each person. Think creatively – consider hardware stores, second-hand shops, craft shops and dime stores for unique presents.

For children, think beyond toys. Consider gifts like art supplies, books and alternatives such as train rides or outings to a museum.

Food First

You can save money if you eat first. Studies show that when you're not hungry, you're a less impulsive and a more careful shopper.

Hands Solo

Do you like to shop with a friend or family member? If so, you may actually be spending more than if you shopped by yourself. According to market research you will buy less if you shop alone.

Stop Before You Drop

When you go shopping, don't overdo it. When exhaustion kicks in, so does impulse buying. The desire to "get it over with" is a strong motivator to buy things outside your budget.

You can save money if you eat before you shop.

Cash Counts

Nothing curbs impulse buying like a wallet without credit cards. Leave your credit card at home and pay cash. Keep a list of all your purchases, so you can review how you spent your money when you get home. When you're finished shopping, total all your receipts and use this amount as a budget for next year. Challenge yourself to spend 10% less the following year.

Give Yourself a Break

If you start feeling stressed, stop what you are doing and take care of yourself. Read something inspirational, call a friend for support or take a break to simply relax and enjoy the essence of the holiday season. Use your budget to keep you financially secure and let your spirit and creativity soar within those parameters.

NOTES

A Closer Look

Learn as They Earn: The Value of Work

The value and pleasure of work.

Remember the first time you did an extra chore or odd job and got paid? Remember the feeling of accomplishment and pride you felt at being grown up enough to have *your own money*?

Helping your children learn the value and pleasure of work increases their confidence, competence and self-esteem. When children work to earn extra money, they build their sense of self-reliance and independence. They also have a chance to increase their skills at:

- Understanding the relationship between time and money

- Recognizing the values of working hard and doing a job well

- Solving problems

- Learning new things

- Listening and following directions

- Understanding money management

- Learning about time management

- Understanding the difference between needs and wants

- Becoming a wise consumer

The Financial Fashion Model

You already model a work ethic by your behavior at home and on the job. You show your children the joys and frustrations of work by the stories you share with them. You also model your system of money management. This includes budgeting, spending, saving and donating money.

Many parents start their kids off early with the idea that money earned can be divided into categories (e.g., spending, saving and donating).

Are you a good financial fashion model?

Some parents simply have three containers for each child. They divide any money the child earns or receives between those three containers in a way that fits with the parents' value system. For example, some families like to donate a percentage, save a percentage and use the rest for spending. Other families will divide the savings category into short-term and long-term savings.

If your child is young, select a system that's easy to implement. If your child is older and you are new to creating such a system, talk to your child about priorities and design a system together that supports your family's values.

What message are you sending your kids about work?

When my children earn or receive any money, 10% goes to tithe, 10% goes to other charities, and 10% goes to their college savings. They're allowed to spend the rest.

Susan, mother of two

$ CFP TIP *The Role Models*

As you talk about work (and that includes working at home, either as a home-based business or a home-based parent), think about what messages you are sending your children. If you portray work as fun, your children will grow up with the notion that work can be fun.

Home Making Money

When they want to earn extra money, start your children's earning careers at home by finding extra work for them to do. Later, you can make suggestions for home-based entrepreneurial ventures (such as a yard work, lemonade stand or car washing) and give them mentoring support. You can also widen their range of potential employers to include family, friends and neighbors.

When you select household chores as a way for your children to earn money, make sure you:

- Select work you'd really like help with.

- Pick work they are capable of doing.

- Communicate clearly what you want done. For example, "clean the bathroom" has many interpretations. Spell or write out exactly what you want completed.

- Agree upon a reasonable deadline.

- Let them know the consequences of not completing the job, such as less or no pay.

- Inspect the job.

- Have them evaluate the job they've done.

Here are some ways other parents have helped their kids earn extra money at home and in their neighborhoods:

The first job my kids had was pet sitting. When a neighbor was out of town they walked the dog and made sure it had food. I supervised everything they did, but made sure I didn't work harder than my children. They also raked leaves, mowed lawns and babysat. These jobs gave them a chance to learn the importance of making a commitment to a job and doing it!

Sharon, mother of two

My son made dog biscuits and sold them to all of our neighbors. He used recipes out of a dog cookbook and tested them on himself and then on his dog. He's quite an entrepreneur. The dog biscuits sold well.

Jodi, mother of three

Pick work they are capable of doing.

My children and a friend decided to raise money for the homeless. They were creative in their fund-raising efforts. They had a lemonade stand several times. They held a car wash in our neighbor's yard. The moms made cookies, and the children sold them. The children put knick-knacks in a box, went into our front yard, played the viola and called to people to stop and buy something from the box. People did. When I had a garage sale, they convinced me to donate the money to the homeless.

They raised more than $150. I took them down to a shelter and we met the director. He listened to their fund-raising tales, gave them a tour of the shelter and answered all their questions.

They could have easily kept the money for themselves, but sharing was more important to them.

Tiffany, mother of two

Don't let them get away with a sloppy job.

CFP TIP   *Chore Power*

Help your kids develop a work ethic by instilling a sense of competence and pride in the chores they do at home. Don't let them get away with a sloppy job. Help them do it right through a loving approach. This builds discipline and pride, traits that can help set them apart as they pursue their careers.

For Better or Worse: Building a Relationship with Work

First, they're madly in love. Then they start noticing problems. Too demanding. Not willing to accept them as they truly are. Not willing to let them use their talents.

"I can't continue this relationship," they tell you. "It's too time consuming. It's not paying off."

So they break up, start looking around. Find a new love on the rebound. This new relationship is much more rewarding. It gives them more freedom and a chance to be creative. It's wonderful again, until they start noticing problems.

A first job is like a first relationship – it's a great learning opportunity. It provides a chance to learn, first hand, about what it means to "work." Your children get to experience the exhilaration, frustration and challenges of working with and for other people. They also get to experience the connection between time and money. They see just how many hours it takes to earn enough money to do the things they want.

When your children express an interest in looking for a job, ask them:

- What type of work would they really like to do?

- How many hours a week do they want to work?

- How will working affect their schoolwork? Do grades have to be maintained at a certain level to keep their job?

- How will they get to and from their job?

- What kinds of ideas or leads do they already have?

- Do they need resumés? If so, do they need help putting them together?

- Do they have the right clothes for the job? If not, how will they get those clothes?

- What kind of help or ideas would they like from you?

What type of work would they really like to do?

In addition to your children pounding the pavement and filling out applications, you may want to use your contacts, friends and networking skills. You can use e-mail to create an e-flyer to send out to people who might be able to offer them a job or share information. You can make phone calls to friends or acquaintances who work in the types of businesses in which your child wants to work. You can ask your family and friends to be on the alert for good opportunities.

Have your kids write down why they think they'll be a good employee.

 CFP TIP *Your Role in Their Job*

You have a vested interest in where your children work. Before they accept any job, introduce yourself to their boss, inspect the working conditions and make sure it's a safe place to work.

When my daughter was looking for a job, I asked her to write down the type of work she wanted and why she thought she'd make a good employee. I emailed her letter to appropriate friends and colleagues. As a result, she got some excellent contacts that led to a good job.

Martha, mother of two

If our teenager wants his own car, we're telling him he must pay for half the initial cost, as well as all insurance and maintenance costs. Faced with this ultimatum, he either has to get a job or face being without wheels. Hopefully, he will also take better care of the vehicle than he would if it were given to him.

Lisa, mother of two

Beyond 9-5

Your child's relationship with work extends beyond simply going there and doing their job. For many kids, this will be their first real interaction with adults in the "outside world." This is an important step to maturity for your child. It also means your role as CFP will take on new dynamics.

Before your child starts his or her first job, have an honest discussion about what's expected in the workplace and what is and isn't appropriate. Explain that some of the people they'll work with might try to take advantage of them by giving them too much responsibility or tasks they're not prepared to do. Encourage your child to be assertive and report any inappropriate behavior or requests to a manager and especially to you.

If your child does come to you with a problem, be open to listening to the child's concern. By listening and talking, you can determine if the job and job situation are right for you child.

 CFP TIP *Teaching Assertiveness*

It's important to teach your children how to be assertive. You can do this by encouraging them to talk about how they feel, what they don't like about a situation and what they want to have happen. For example, if asked to lock-up a store at the end of the day, your child could say, "I feel nervous about locking-up at the end of the day. I've never done it before and don't know for sure how to do it. Will someone do it with me for the first week to be sure I do it right." If their employer tries to convince them otherwise, your child should acknowledge what the employer said and then repeat this type of dialogue until they get their desired response.

MONEY MATTERS

Some of the reasons teens want to work are:

- *To develop a feeling of independence and a sense of responsibility*

- *To buy clothes*

- *To be independent of parents*

A Closer Look

Pay Yourself First®

Pay yourself first.®

I f you want to help ensure your financial security or if you have a long-term financial goal in mind, like saving for your child's education or your retirement, it helps to have an investment plan.

One way to make your long-term goals a reality is to make a commitment to Pay Yourself First.® That means, before you pay your monthly bills, before you set aside money for vacation or a new car, before you go out to eat or to a movie, your first commitment each month should be to yourself.

There was always something that seemed more pressing and more important than investing for retirement. It was more satisfying to get new carpet or the latest computer. Saving money for retirement just wasn't a priority. Finally, it dawned on us, we have to save for retirement, too. So, my wife and I both went to an automatic investment system. Now the money is invested directly from our paychecks, before we can dream of ways to spend them.

Colin, father of three

Invest Regularly

Many families find it easier to save for their long-term goals by making automatic investments. With an automatic investment, you always Pay Yourself First, thereby keeping your financial future a top priority.

Here's how it works:

Each month, you arrange to have a set amount of money deducted from your paycheck or withdrawn from a bank account and directly deposited into an investment vehicle of your choosing. The easiest way to stay committed to automatic investments

---

MONEY MATTERS

One survey estimates that two-thirds of the workforce has not calculated how much income they'll need for retirement.

Employee Benefit Research Institute survey

---

is to make deposits on a regular schedule with a fixed dollar amount. For example, you may decide to contribute $100 on the 15th of each month to a college account for your child.

Some common methods of automatic investing include:

- Deductions from a personal checking or savings account

- Direct deposits from your paycheck

- Direct deposits from other sources, such as military allotments or Social Security payments

- Contributing to an employer retirement plan, such as a 401(k), by payroll deduction (this is one of the most common methods of automatic investing)

Many financial institutions, mutual fund companies and brokerage firms offer an automatic investment or direct deposit service for savings or investment accounts. Sometimes you must meet a minimum investment requirement before you can start investing automatically. If you plan to open a new account, always be sure to review the company's policy.

Take Advantage of Time

There are several advantages to automatic investing:

- **It's convenient.** Since the investments occur automatically, you don't have to worry about mailing a check each month or losing the opportunity because you spent the money elsewhere.

- **You keep your long-term plans on track** by investing regularly, regardless of what is happening in the financial markets. It may be tempting to stop investing when market conditions are unstable or unfavorable. But successful investments are more likely to be the result of time in – not timing of – the stock and bond markets.

MONEY MATTERS

Many families review their retirement budget at least once a year. Because you'll be looking at your financial documents, one of the best times to do this is while you're preparing your taxes.

- **You eliminate the guesswork of investing.** When you invest on a regular basis, you will buy more shares when the price is low and fewer shares when the price is high. This can lower your overall average cost per share. By consistently investing at regular intervals, you can "ride-out" fluctuations in the market. This is frequently called "dollar cost averaging." Dollar cost averaging helps take the guesswork and emotion out of investing in the market. However, dollar-cost averaging does not ensure a profit and does not protect you against loss in declining markets.

Commit to the Long-Term: Coping with Downturns and Upswings

We were confused. The market went way down and our nest egg was the size of a quail egg. Rather than panic and pull out, we decided to tough it out and stay in. It's hard to do, but we believe investing is a long-term process.

Lana, mother of two

Review Your Goals

If you're trying to determine if this is a good time to start an automatic investment plan, review your current financial situation to see whether you can allocate money toward your goal.

Many financial planners suggest that you invest at least 10% of your annual gross income. For example, if your salary is $30,000, you should plan on investing $3,000 a year.

You can better ride-out fluctuations in the market by investing at regular intervals.

If, however, you don't feel you can afford to invest the suggested 10% a year, don't let that discourage you. Even if you can invest as little as $50 per month, you will still be closer to achieving your goal than if you invest nothing at all. You may find an opportunity to start automatic investments when you receive a promotion, a pay raise at work or when you pay off a car loan or other debt.

You may also have opportunities to invest in addition to automatic investments. For example, you may want to make an extra investment if you receive a tax refund or a bonus check from your employer.

It's a good idea to review your investment portfolio, including automatic investments, at least once a year. You may need to change the amount of your automatic investment or reallocate investments if you have more than one account.

Even If You Don't Have Much, Invest Something

Sometimes, everything can be going along smoothly with your long-term investment plans, and then something changes – you get laid off; your position gets downsized; or one of you decides to become a stay-at-home parent and your income decreases. Regardless of the circumstances, try to continue to pay yourself first every month. Even modest amounts can add up. The psychological advantage of knowing you are taking care of yourself can add a sense of confidence to your life.

No Borrowing from the Cookie Jar

If you find yourself without a job or with a reduced income and have to temporarily stop making your regular monthly investments, try not to borrow from your long-term savings. Disrupting these funds can reduce your long-term financial stability and decrease your chances of meeting your long-term goals. If you're changing jobs, consider rolling-over your retirement savings into an IRA, where the money will keep its tax-deferred status. This can give you more choice and control over your money than if it stayed in your former employer's 401(k).

Sometimes, everything can be going along smoothly with your long-term investment plans, and then something changes...

The Golden Years, the Platinum Expenses

It's easy to imagine one day spending your time traveling, pursuing hobbies and enjoying a more leisurely life. It's harder to figure out just what this life will cost you.

If you want to maintain your current lifestyle when you are retired, some experts advise having 70% to 80% of your current annual income for each year. For example, if your current annual income is $40,000, you'll probably need $28,000 to $32,000 annually to maintain your current standard of living in retirement. Of course, your estimated income will vary with your lifestyle. It's quite possible to choose a modest lifestyle and live on much less.

First, figure out what your retirement income will be. You can calculate this by adding up all your retirement income sources. These may include:

- Your 401(k)

- Other employer retirement plans

- Social Security payments

- Interest on investments

Next, consider your current expenses and think about how they may change after you retire. Of course, your parenting-related expenses will change. You may choose to live in a smaller or a different home. You may spend more on entertainment and health care and less on items such as clothing or vehicles.

The following list can help you start planning your retirement expenses:

- Taxes (federal and state, real estate, personal property)

- Real Estate (mortgage payments, insurance, maintenance, second-home costs)

- Utilities (electric, gas, water, trash, phone, cable/satellite, Internet)

- Vehicles (loan payments, insurance, license, maintenance)

MONEY MATTERS

According to a survey from American Century Investments, one-third of all workers would consider taking money from their retirement savings if they lost their jobs, despite the fact that they could lose up to half of their money in taxes and penalties.

- Health Care (medical insurance, out-of-pocket costs, prescriptions, glasses, vitamins)

- Personal Care (toiletries, cosmetics, haircuts)

- Food (groceries)

- Clothing (new clothes, laundry soap, dry cleaning, tailoring)

- Vacations (travel, lodging, food, entertainment, souvenirs)

- Entertainment (restaurants, tickets, movie rentals, books, CDs)

- Savings/Contributions (charities, education savings)

- Memberships/Licenses (golf or health clubs, social clubs, professional organizations)

- Miscellaneous (gifts, magazines, newspapers)

Once you compare your estimated income and expenses, you'll be able to see if you're on track for retirement. If not, revisit your family budget and look for ways you can spend less so you can increase your monthly retirement savings.

You can also use the Stowers Financial Analysis to help you determine how much money you will need and how much you should start saving today. A copy of this CD-ROM can be obtained through the Stowers Innovations, Inc. Web site at www.stowers-innovations.com.

 CFP TIP   *The Better Third*

Many people spend up to one-third of their lives in retirement, so it's important to plan carefully for the lifestyle you want. Otherwise, you may run out of money.

NOTES

It's quite possible to choose a modest lifestyle
and live on much less.

A Closer Look

Educate Yourself About College Plans and Savings

Sending your kid to college can be a barrel of fun.

If paying for your child's college education (or at least helping to pay for it) is important to you, you'll need to determine how much it will cost and how to go about paying for it.

Know What You're Looking At

Imagine a tall building that keeps adding floors. That's the story of college costs – they just keep going up, beyond the rate of inflation. Historically, college costs have risen an average of about 5% a year. At that rate, a child in kindergarten in 2004 will need more than $104,000 for four years of tuition and expenses at an in-state public college or nearly $225,000 for a private college.

Now is the Time ...

We started saving for their college education the minute we found out I was pregnant!

Sharon, mother of three

The earlier you begin investing for your child's education, the more time your college savings or investments have to grow. Starting your savings plan in conjunction with the birth of your child is not only ideal, it's the easiest solution for your pocket book.

If you put off starting your college savings until your child is older, you can still reach your goals; however, you will have to invest more money per month to do it. For example, if you start investing when your child is four, you will need to increase your savings by 50% per month. If you start when your child is in the eighth grade, you'll need to save three times more per month. Remember, time is one of your most powerful allies when investing.

> ### MONEY MATTERS
>
> *In 2002-2003, public colleges and universities raised tuition and fees by an average of almost 10%.*

Give Your Kids the Responsibility

Even though both of us had to work our way through college, we want to pay for at least half of our kids' college education. That's why we started saving for their college before our first child was born. Because we paid our own way, we had a strong sense of accomplishment. We want our children to experience that same feeling.

Stephen, father of two

"It's not just the tuition – It's the room and board that are the shockers."

Some parents encourage their children to save a little for college as soon as they can earn chore money. Some parents give matching funds for any funds their children save. Other families require their kids to put a percentage of monies earned or received in a college fund.

Get the Gift of Education

When the kids were little, we encouraged relatives to give savings bonds or contribute to a savings account rather than shower the kids with gifts they didn't really need. Now each of our children has money in savings. When they're older and want to go to college, they will have some money set aside to help pay for some of the expenses.

Darlene, mother of three

It's important to understand that young children are not small adults. Until they reach the teen years, it's best not to overload children with the financial concerns of college. By the time kids reach age 13, they've had enough life experiences to begin to understand the responsibilities ahead of them. Putting too much financial pressure on kids at a young age can be difficult for them to deal with.

$ CFP TIP *Educational Fund-Raising*

One family had a simple plan to pay for college. They asked their close friends and family to go light on the adorable baby gifts and make monetary gifts to their child's college fund. Through the years, they've insisted that their daughter contribute a portion of any financial gifts she gets to the fund. Sixteen years later, that fund is now the basis for their daughter's college education.

Choosing the Right Course of Investments

It's no secret that the key to saving enough for college is to start investing early.

Some parents invest a lump sum when their child is born and never touch that account until college time.

Money invested at an average annual return of 5% when your child is born will more than double in value by the time they're college age.

Other parents prefer to start with a smaller initial investment and then add to it on a regular basis.

Once you determine how much you can invest and how often you can add to that investment, you will be better prepared to choose an investment plan. Many tax-advantaged investment plans for college exist, including: 529 Plans, Coverdell Education Savings Accounts (CESA), Unified Gift to Minor Act (UGMA), Unified Trust to Minor Act (UTMA), Traditional IRA and Roth IRA.

The chart on the following pages will help you compare the advantages and disadvantages of the investment plans so you can choose the plan that best suits your needs.

MONEY MATTERS

One of the biggest financial challenges your kids will face in college is the temptation of credit cards.

	529 Plans	**CESA** [1]
Who controls or owns the account?	Account owner (may be the student). controls the account.	Parent or guardian until the child reaches a set age, unless the parent or guardian elects to retain control.
How can I use the money?	Must be used to pay qualified expenses at an eligible educational institution to avoid income and penalty taxes.	Must be used for qualified education expenses before the student reaches age 30 to avoid penalty.
Are there contribution limits?	Yes, although maximum contribution limits vary from state 529 Plan to state 529 Plan. However, a 529 Plan allows for much higher contributions than other education savings options – often upwards of $200,000 per beneficiary.	Yes. $2,000 per year until child reaches age 18.
Does my income level limit my contributions?	No.	Yes. Eligibility begins to phase out at $95,000 AGI ($190,000 AGI for taxpayers filing jointly).
How will the account be taxed?	Taxes on earnings are deferred until withdrawn. The earnings portion of qualified withdrawals are free from federal income taxes[3]. No federal gift tax on contributions for each student up to $55,000 per contributor ($110,000 for spousal gifts) in one year if contributor recognizes that gift over five years for tax purposes.	Qualified withdrawals are exempt from federal income tax. State tax treatment may vary.
What are the penalties for non-qualified use?	Earnings are taxed as ordinary income and are subject to penalty.	Withdrawals on earnings are taxed as ordinary income and a penalty tax may apply.
Can I change the beneficiary?	Yes. Transfer to another qualified member of the student's family is allowed without a penalty tax.	Yes. In some cases, a transfer to another family member is allowed without penalty.
Other considerations:	Contributions to a CESA and 529 Plan are allowed in the same year for the same student.	Contributions to a CESA and 529 Plan are allowed in the same year for the same student. A CESA may be transferred to a 529 Plan.

Investment plans comparison provided courtesy of American Century Investments – 2003. (1) The Coverdell Education Savings Account (CESA), formerly known as an Education IRA.

This is for informational purposes only and is not intended as investment advice.

UGMA / UTMA [2]	Traditional IRAs	Roth IRAs
The money belongs to the child. A custodian controls the money until the child reaches a set age, which varies by state.	Account owner.	Account owner.
Money used before the child is a set age must be used for the child's benefit. After that, the child controls the money.	May be used for qualified higher education expenses.	May be used for qualified higher education expenses.
There is no lifetime limit.	Yes. $3,000 per person per year in 2002-2004. $4,000 per year in 2005-2007. $5,000 in 2008, then indexed for inflation in $500 increments. Taxpayers 50 and older are allowed higher limits to "catch-up" on their savings. [3] Depends on the type of IRA.	Yes. $3,000 per year in 2002-2004. $4,000 per year in 2005-2007. $5,000 in 2008, then indexed for inflation in $500 increments. Taxpayers 50 and older are allowed higher limits to "catch-up" on their savings. [3]
No.	There is no income limit for a non-deductible IRA. Deductible IRA subject to eligibility phase out.	Yes. Eligibility begins to phase out at $95,000 AGI ($150,000 AGI for taxpayers filing jointly).
Some investment earnings may be exempt from federal income tax; some may be taxed at the child's and/or parent's rate. Contributions larger than $11,000 a year may be subject to gift tax (annual gift exclusion amount subject to adjustment). With changing tax laws, this amount may be adjusted. State tax treatment may vary.	Withdrawals before age 59 1/2 may be subject to taxes and penalty tax. Qualified education expenses are not subject to penalty tax.	Withdrawals of contributions are allowed anytime. Withdrawals of earnings before age 59 1/2 may be subject to income taxes and penalty tax. Qualified education expenses are not subject to penalty tax.
Not applicable.	Withdrawals of earnings and deductible contributions are taxed as ordinary income, and a 10% early withdrawal penalty tax may apply before age 59 1/2 may be subject to taxes and penalty.	Withdrawals of earnings may be taxed as ordinary income and a 10% early withdrawal penalty tax may apply.
No. The money belongs to the child.	Not applicable to higher education.	Not applicable to higher education.
Transfer of a UGMA or UTMA account to a 529 Plan is allowed but may be subject to income tax.	If money is not used for qualified education expenses, it may be withdrawn penalty-free beginning at age 59 1/2. Required distributions begin at age 70 1/2.	If money is not used for qualified education expenses, earnings may be withdrawn tax free once the five-year rule has been met and penalty free at age 59 1/2.

(2) The Uniform Gifts and Uniform Transfers to Minors Acts. (3) Changes resulting from the Tax Relief Act of 2001 are effective through December 31, 2010, and may be extended past that date with further legislative action.

CFP TIP *How to Choose a 529 Plan*

Analyze a 529 Plan as you would any investment:

- *Look at the investment management partner and analyze the plan's track record.*

- *Look at tax advantages, but these are secondary to fund performance.*

- *Look at plans from other states and see what advantages, performance wise, they might offer.*

- *Look into how the plan might affect your child's chances of financial aid. A 529 Plan counts as assets of the account owner.*

Money Matters

You can contribute to a CESA and a 529 Plan during the same year for the same student.

Planning is key to everything when it comes to preparing for college. Even before your child gets to high school, start looking at colleges and find out their requirements. Then, you can encourage your child to take the right high school classes to get into the college of their choice. This is also a good time to start looking at scholarships to get an idea of what has to be done in order to qualify.

Ayeesha, mother of two

Don't Have Enough? Don't Despair!

If you have a child nearing college age, but don't think your savings or investments will cover your costs, all is not lost. Colleges, after all, do not require that you have cash to cover the entire tuition and fees before your child is allowed to enter. If you are in this situation, you are not alone. Many parents use more of a "shotgun" approach when paying for college; paying part from their current income, taking advantage of student loans, taking out a home equity line of credit and using their savings or investments.

We may pay off our house early and then borrow against our home to help finance college. Or we may sell our home, move into a smaller home and use the extra money to help finance college.

George, father of three

Financial Assistance

Student financial assistance programs are a valuable resource to consider when paying for college. Many students are eligible for some sort of financial aid. How much will depend on many factors. Unless the school provides a student scholarship, you or your child will be responsible for paying back the aid.

First Things First

In most instances, before you can apply for financial assistance, you and your child must first complete the Free Application for Federal Student Aid, more commonly referred to as the FAFSA. The federal government uses the information provided on the FAFSA to determine your Expected Family Contribution (EFC), which is the amount they expect the student and his or her family to contribute to educational expenses.

You may complete and submit the FAFSA online at www.fafsa.ed.gov. You can also obtain a copy of this from your child's high school counseling office, a college or university financial aid office, or by calling 1-800-433-3243.

It is important that you submit the FAFSA as soon as possible after January 1 and after you figure your income taxes during your child's senior year of high school.

Once the FAFSA is processed, you will receive a Student Aid Report (SAR). This report will also be sent to the college or university of your choice. Your school will then determine the types and amounts of financial aid for which your student is eligible and your options. You will also receive information that will help you with the application process.

You or your child are responsible for paying back financial aid.

Loans

Some families may choose to take out a loan to pay for college. Depending on your circumstances, you and your child may qualify for any number of student or parent loans. Because the rules governing these loans may change, we encourage you to search the Internet or library for information about:

- Federal Perkins loans for students
- Stafford student loans
- Parent Loan for Undergraduate Students (PLUS)
- PELL Grants

Before You Sign On the Dotted Line ...

You are signing a contract when you accept financial aid. Read it carefully. Pay close attention to the interest rate and terms and conditions of the loan.

Here are some important things to keep in mind when taking out a college loan:

- When you take out a loan, you are making a promise that you will pay it back. That means even if your child doesn't graduate, isn't able to get a job after graduation, or is dissatisfied with the education received, the full amount of the loan must still be paid back.

- Think about the terms of repaying your loan before you accept it. There could be serious consequences if you don't pay back the loan when it's due. These consequences include damaging your credit rating which could prevent other lenders from loaning you money in the future.

- You must make your loan payments, even if you don't receive a bill or repayment reminder. Unlike a credit card which offers you the option of making a "minimum payment amount," your monthly payments are due in the full amount agreed upon in your repayment plan. Partial payments won't do.

MONEY MATTERS

If your kids go away to college and leave their cars at home, they may qualify for substantial discounts on insurance.

Other Courses of Action

You still have many options to help your child manage the high cost of college besides savings, investments and loans.

Scholarships

Scholarships are open to students who need financial help and those who otherwise might not qualify for financial aid. They are granted on a wide variety of criteria including academics, class rank, financial need, leadership qualities, athletic ability, creativity and community service.

Although many companies will offer to help you locate scholarships for a fee, you can easily find them yourself on the Internet. A simple search using the keywords "college scholarship" will provide hundreds of links to choose from. Scholarship information should also be available through your child's high school counselor.

Grants

Grants are available from the federal government, trade organizations and individual companies. Unlike a loan, grant money typically does not have to be repaid. However, the provider of the grant may require your child to make a commitment to a certain course of study or career choice.

To qualify for a grant, your child may have to complete a lengthy essay questionnaire and maintain a high academic standing. To find a listing of available grants on the Internet, do a search using the keywords "college grant." You can also check with your local library for additional direction and information.

Scholarships are awarded for a wide variety of criteria.

Work/Study

Work/study jobs give part-time employment to undergraduate and graduate students who need income to help meet the costs of post-secondary education. This can complement the student's educational program or offer relevant work experience in a business setting.

Unlike other types of financial aid, work/study is paid directly to the student as it is earned. There are usually a wide variety of work/study positions available both on and off campus with schedules designed to meet the needs of the student.

In most cases, either the Financial Aid Office or the Office of Student Employment at your child's college or university will determine eligibility and allocate work/study funds to students.

Work/study jobs help students earn while they learn.

Stay Home and Save

For some kids, college is not complete if they don't leave home. But for others, a college education can be found, often more economically, in their own backyard. Some good options are attending a community college or a local college while living at home.

We knew we wouldn't have enough to send our son away to school. We learned that the community college near us was one of the best in the country. We told our son if he was successful during his two years there, we'd help him go away to school for the final two years. The community college was perfect for him and for us. He loved his classes, poured himself into work and study, and he still had time to have fun. We got to help our son get a college education without going into major debt.

George, father of two

Community colleges can provide students with an excellent and less-costly education. Most offer both applied degrees, which qualify the student for a job immediately after graduation, or transfer degrees, so the student can move on to a four-year college or university to complete a bachelor's degree.

In addition to saving on tuition, attending a local college means your child can live at home. That means you can save on room and board. Depending on the school and amenities, room and board can typically run from $4,000 to well over $7,000 a year.

NOTES

A Closer Look

Life Insurance

Life insurance can be one of the more confusing

family financial issues.

P erhaps you've experienced this scenario: You're interested in buying life insurance, but you don't know exactly what kind you want or if you even need it. You call a friend who's a life insurance agent and ask for advice.

He begins to throw around phrases like "whole life," "universal life," and "variable life." Then he starts talking about cross-purchasing, premiums, convertible terms and lapse termination. Your eyes glaze over. The only thing you know for certain after you talk is that you have a headache. You still don't know what to do about life insurance.

Come to Terms with Life Insurance

Life insurance can be one of the more confusing family financial issues. Yet life insurance is also the ultimate emergency reserve fund. If something should happen to you or your spouse, the right life insurance policy can make a significant difference to the surviving spouse and children.

When Do You Need Life Insurance?

When we first had children, we bought a $200,000 annual renewable term life insurance policy on my life. This type of policy provided the most protection for the least amount of money.

James Stowers

Life insurance is something every parent should consider … no matter what your age. Even if you are a healthy person, born of a long line of healthy people, accidents happen. To fully protect your family, you'll want to consider life insurance.

"Insurance doesn't need to be expensive if you buy the right kind."

James Stowers

Who you buy your insurance from is as important as what type of insurance you buy.

When Bob told me he wanted to buy life insurance, I thought he was crazy. We were both strong and healthy. I wanted to put the money into a vacation fund so we could take our two grade school age daughters on a trip. But Bob prevailed – he really wanted insurance. Three years later, I was grateful for his proactive thinking. When he was killed in an accident, one thing I didn't have to worry about immediately was money. The life insurance served as a foundation for us. It helped us keep our house and car, even during those months when I was so sad I couldn't work.

Donna, mother of two

What Kind of Life Insurance is Best for You?

Sometimes the best insurance can be the least expensive. One of the least expensive is ***Pure Permanent Annual Renewable Term***.

Pure Permanent Annual Renewable Term life insurance gives you only life insurance protection. It has no cash value. The "permanent" part means the insurance is guaranteed to be renewable for life. You only pay the increased mortality cost to the insurance company.

$ CFP TIP *Investing Your Insurance Savings*

*If you buy **Pure Permanent Annual Renewable Term** life insurance, you should consider wisely investing any money you save by switching from the other policy.*

How Much Do You Need?

The purpose of life insurance is not to make your surviving family instant millionaires. It's to replace the loss of your income for a period of time necessary to assure your family doesn't endure any unnecessary hardships.

If you died today, how much money would your family need? To come up with an answer, you need to consider the following factors:

How do you want your family to live?

If you were to suddenly die, how would you want your family to continue living? Would you want them to continue living in the same home? Would you expect your spouse to continue guiding your children toward your mutual goals and dreams? Consider all the things you would want your family to be able to do, even if you weren't in the picture. Then, think about how much money they would need to live the way you'd like them to.

How much income does your family need each month?

Use the budget outline in Chapter Three to help you determine your monthly expenses (keep in mind, some of those costs might be reduced if you aren't there). Assuming your family continues to live in the same house and their monthly living costs remain essentially the same, write down how much they'll need each month. Next, factor in your monthly contributions to your college savings plan, your emergency fund and any investments you want to continue. Finally, determine if health insurance comes from your work. If it does, then factor in an additional monthly cost for health insurance.

Total the numbers. This is the amount of money your family will need each month to continue their current lifestyle and plans. If you are married with a working spouse, then subtract from the total the amount of income your spouse earns each month. This new number is the amount of money your life insurance policy should provide on a monthly basis.

> ### MONEY MATTERS
>
> *Look for a top rated insurance company that has at least an "A" rating.*

MONEY MATTERS

Take care of your health.

Many insurance companies

offer discounts to people

who live healthy lifestyles.

If you smoke, you can expect

to pay a higher premium

than if you are a non-smoker.

Another way to determine the amount of insurance you need is to look at the amount of gross income you earn and multiply it from five to 10 times. For example, if your gross income is $35,000 – then you may want to get a policy that pays a benefit of $175,000 to $350,000.

Combined with the surviving spouse's income, this amount should be enough to:

- Feed, dress and educate your kids

- Pay off any debts you and your spouse have, that your spouse wouldn't be able to pay off on his or her own

- Cover the estimated funeral costs and any other costs associated with dying

By doing these calculations and selecting the amount of term life insurance you need, you give your family the financial security they need to continue to live without assuming a financial burden. Because it's the least expensive, term life also helps you save money, which you can invest in your goals and dreams.

The process of being self-insured.

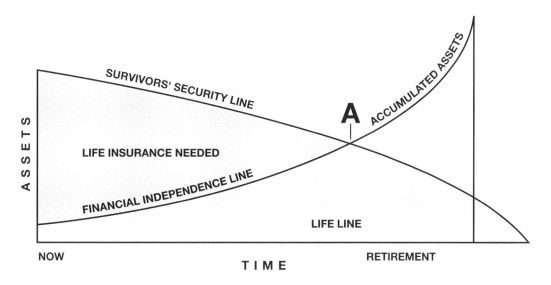

CFP TIP   *The Law of Diminishing Need*

As your children get older, your survivors' security needs should diminish. Once your kids are out of college and on their own, you don't need as much life insurance. At some point, you may not even need life insurance because your accumulated assets are greater than your calculated insurance needs. At this point ("A" in the graph above), you're "self-insured."

Part 2

A Closer Look

Spending Time Without Spending Lots of Money

Any amount of quality "family time" is priceless in their eyes.

Do you feel as though you spend enough time having fun with your children? Are you often torn between work, household duties and family time? A recent poll commissioned by the Center for the New American Dream showed that 60% of the children surveyed said they'd rather spend time having fun with their parents than shopping at the mall. A majority of the kids surveyed wanted to change their parents' jobs so Mom and Dad could spend more time doing fun family activities.

Some of the best time you can spend with your kids happens without planning. *You're sitting at the kitchen table reviewing a document for work. Your child comes in and just starts talking to you.*

Is this an interruption or a golden opportunity to share a special moment? How you react will help define your relationship with your child and the values you want to instill. Why not make this a special moment? Take time out from your work. Get down at your child's level so you're looking eye-to-eye. Use a soft voice to discuss and admire what he or she has to share. After a while, you both go back to what you were doing.

Without spending a penny, you've just created an experience that will go a long way to raising a happy child filled with love and self-esteem.

No matter how much time you spend with your kids, any amount of quality "family time" is priceless in their eyes. To help you spend a lot of time without spending a lot of money, we've gathered some other wonderful ideas for you and your children to share.

Spend more time doing fun family activities.

CFP TIP   *Preparing for Family Time*

- *Turn off the phone*
- *Forget the newspaper*
- *Reach out to your children*

- *Turn off the computer and TV*
- *Put your chores and errands on hold*
- *Go play*

Finding Home Town Fun

Be a tourist in your own town. Once you start looking for inexpensive, fascinating experiences, you will find an abundance of ideas and events.

Here are some easy ways to get started:

- Look in your local paper for free events.
- Check with local museums and attractions about events that might be of special interest. Also find out which days are free.
- Contact your local library for a schedule of events.
- Keep an eye open for bookstore offerings and author events.
- Watch for family activities sponsored by local community centers, hospitals and community colleges.
- Talk with the parents of your kid's friends and see what types of activities they enjoy doing together.
- Look for musical, artistic or spiritual events hosted by religious groups.
- Get a schedule from your parks and recreation department.
- Surf the Internet for fun or unusual things to do in your area.
- Contact your Chamber of Commerce or Convention and Visitors Bureau and ask for local tour and visitor's information.

Create a play space where a certain amount of tumble and noise is welcome.

$ CFP TIP   *Make Your Home Kid Central*

How do you get to be "kid central?" If you like to have your children and their friends stay close to home, create a comfortable play space. Have artistic and other easy activities for them and a place where a certain amount of tumble and noise is welcome. Be willing to share soft drinks and treats. As they get older, you can keep them coming back by converting this area into a game room or TV room.

The Grand Outdoors

You don't need to have anything planned to enjoy being outdoors with your children. You can just go outside, either into your yard, on a walk or to a nearby park and see what unfolds. Part of the fun is giving your kids unstructured play time (and giving yourself some as well).

Here are some ideas for those times when you need something new:

Clue In

Go on a "detective walk." Look for objects on the ground that might serve as clues. You can look for either natural things, such as interesting rocks or twigs, or "found" objects, such as scraps of paper with handwriting on them, ribbons or abandoned toys. Pick up these clues as you walk and weave together an entertaining story. You may want to wear gloves or take along waterless anti-bacterial soap, too.

Go to the Dogs

Many local parks have areas where dogs can run free. Take your children and your dog, if you have one, and mingle with the other dogs and owners. It's a treat to see all kinds of interesting dogs and meet their owners. If you don't have your own dog, you can still go watch the dogs play. Or, go with a friend who has a dog.

If you don't have your own dog, you can go watch other dogs play.

Silent Morning

Plan a morning of solitude to enjoy the silence and beauty. Get up early and watch the sun come up. You may want to go to a park, or a place of quiet natural beauty. Don't talk. Just enjoy the quiet and notice the natural sounds you hear. You can also have a simple picnic breakfast of fruit and muffins while you spend time just being in nature.

Patch Work

While at a park or in your own yard, have your children find their own small patch of ground. Notice the temperature, texture, color, and odors. Make a list of all the things they see in that patch of ground. Share with them how you would have walked right past these things if you hadn't slowed down.

A Play Fair

Get a couple of families together to play a sport, such as baseball, kickball, volleyball or basketball.

The Playground Tour

Become playground experts. Take your children to different playgrounds. Create a name for each playground and rate it based on several factors like size, equipment, distance from home and overall fun. After you've visited several, help your child create a report or a map to share with classmates.

Wheel Easy

All over the country, cities and counties are encouraging families to explore the great outdoors by creating hiking and biking trails. Find some trails near your house and head out on your bikes or on foot for a nature walk. Be sure to take time to stop and look at all of the wonders of nature along the route.

Spend time just being in nature.

Rolling Down the Water

Theme parks often have reciprocal passes for other parks across the country. If you have a theme park near you, calculate the cost of getting a season pass. If you intend to travel to another city that has a park that will honor your pass, you may be able to save a lot of money.

One family planned their vacation around different theme parks in the region. By buying a reciprocal pass at one they got in all of the others for "free."

Adventure Without Upkeep

For a small amount of money you can buy recreational items that don't cost you additional money in upkeep or usage. Depending on the interests of your family, consider canoes, sailboats, skates, bicycles or tents.

Digging the Time Together

Gardening is a great family activity. You get the fun of playing in dirt with the reward of growing something beautiful or edible. Here are some ways to have fun gardening together:

- Have your child pick a package of seeds. Find a special place and help your child sprout them.

- Ask your children to come with you to help an elderly neighbor in his or her garden.

- Get a plot in a community garden – as a family, plant a flower or vegetable garden.

- Volunteer to help beautify a local park, by either weeding, planting or picking up trash.

Gardening also provides an excellent educational opportunity to talk to your kids about how plants grow, as well as learning to fulfill a commitment to care for the plants.

Have your child pick a package of seeds. Find a special place and help your child sprout them.

Kitchen Made

The kitchen is a great place to connect with your kids and teach them a valuable life skill. One mom had every Friday night as "someone else cook dinner" night. One of her children would choose the menu and prepare the dinner, with assistance as needed. This kitchen time was so popular that her son later became a chef.

When you plan activities in the kitchen, choose times when you are relaxed and not in a rush. If you want to teach your children about cooking, pick recipes they will enjoy preparing and eating. Try to eliminate distractions and make this a time for talking and creating.

This is a great way to help your kids feel comfortable in the kitchen. The kitchen experience includes cooking survival skills, the culinary arts, parent-child bonding and fun. In addition, you often turn out something delicious to eat.

A Recipe for Delicious Fun

Choose some dishes your children love eating. Then invite your kids to help you with what you need to cook. According to their ages and abilities, have them chop and stir with you. Ask them to mix and knead. Throw in a little instruction and direction. Then relax and let the conversation flow while the meal cooks. Enjoy the process, as well as the product.

Some children may even enjoy the idea of baking their own birthday cake.

The Icing's On

For extra fun, invite your children to help you decorate cakes, cupcakes or cookies. Encourage them to be creative. Provide different colors of frosting and different toppings, such as candy-coated chocolates, sprinkles or crumbled cookies. This is a fun way to spend an afternoon. Some children may even enjoy the idea of baking their own birthday cake.

Carry Out

Bake a dessert for a neighbor, friend or for a good cause. This is a chance to combine culinary creativity with good deeds. Plus, if you're giving your dessert away, it's fewer calories for all of you.

Housing Authorities

Create a gingerbread house with your kids. Use graham crackers, and "glue" the house together. Invite your child to decorate the house using all kinds of candies and cookies. You can even create a window with plastic wrap. Leave the back of the house open and put a low watt light bulb inside, for a warm, homey glow. This may sound like an activity only for the little ones, but often when older kids see how much fun it is, they'll want their own house!

Into the Drink

Want to be on equal footing in the kitchen? Want to challenge your willingness to try new things? If your answers are yes, you're ready for Weird Drink Night.

Here's how it works. Put a variety of beverages on the counter. Everyone gets to create one weird drink from a concoction of these liquids, using as many different liquids as they wish. Only one rule: the creator of the drink has to be willing to take the first sip of what they create. Invite everyone to name his or her drink and see if you're willing to try each one.

One family did this as an activity during a Halloween party. In addition to different beverages, they included table condiments like ketchup, mustard, salt and pepper.

Weird drink night.

> **RECIPE: Gingerbread House "Glue"**
>
> With an electric mixer, beat 3 large egg whites and 1 teaspoon of water until frothy. Add 1 teaspoon cream of tartar and beat until whites are stiff, but not dry. Mix in 3 cups sifted powdered sugar; beat on high speed for about 5 minutes. It should be of spreading consistency. Use immediately or keep tightly covered and refrigerated for up to 8 hours.

CFP TIP   *Construction Favors*

Building gingerbread houses makes a fun and easy party theme. The kids then get to take home their finished houses as their party favor.

Creative Explorations - Books, Arts, Culture and More

The arts are a wonderful part of life. Exploring words, music and art together invites your children to widen their interests and expand their creativity.

Go for the Culture

Join a zoo, museum or similar group. For a small initial payment, you gain access and reduced price or free entry. It encourages you to make use of these wonderful cultural resources. Ask about reciprocal agreements with other museums. Some science museum memberships are good for museums throughout the country.

For a small initial fee, you can join a zoo.

Book Worms

Read out loud. Kids love to have stories read to them. In the summertime, go outside. Some families have an ongoing story they read every night, or one night a week. Some families read a short prayer or inspirational story before meals. Choose a variety of books, including the classic books that kids like and understand but might not read on their own. Or read books that excite historical interest, such as the ***Little House on the Prairie*** series.

Reading to your children can help you relax. The experience also gives you a common story to refer to and talk about.

CFP TIP   *The Art of the Familiar*

Make the gallery experience a scavenger hunt. Ask your kids to look for colors, animals, fruit or familiar objects as you look at the art.

Reading from the Same Page

Start a book club, either with friends, family or a combination. Mother-daughter and father-son book clubs are popular. This is a great way to connect with your child, be with other like-minded parents and children, and get to know each other through reading and discussing. If you're starting a club, ask your child who they'd like to have join. Then call their friends' parents and see if you can find a time to get together.

You can either select a book in advance to start discussing at your first meeting, or get together as a group, select the books, and decide how you want the group to operate.

For a great reference look for ***The Mother-Daughter Book Club: How Ten Busy Mothers and Daughters Came Together to Talk, Laugh and Learn Through Their Love of Reading*** by Shireen Dodson and Teresa Barker.

Click Your Heels Together

Try folk dancing. Most community centers offer some sort of dancing lessons. Most of the dances are fairly easy to learn and the groups can be very kid friendly. In fact, the children often turn out to be among the best dancers. This is a great way to exercise and learn about teamwork and cooperation while becoming part of a group. You also hear great music, meet good people and have fun.

Kids love to have stories read to them.

Listening to Joyful Noises

Outdoor community theater and concerts are usually family friendly places. The kids can watch, run or sleep. They get to experience the theater and music while you get an evening out.

Recycled Art

Create art projects from recycled materials. First have a scavenger hunt for the materials. Look around your home and see what you could turn into art. Twist ties, bottle tops, newspapers, toilet paper rolls … take an artist's tour and then create.

Craft and Arts

Get a book that lists crafts you can make and let the kids select a craft project you can do together. Or, go to a craft store and let your kids pick out a kit, then work on the project together.

 CFP TIP *Kid Friendly Hobbies*

To help create a lifetime of memories together, look for hobbies that are kid friendly. For example, model railroading, kite flying, scrapbooking, jigsaw puzzles and building doll houses all provide opportunities for your children to participate in some way.

Create art projects from recycled materials.

Creative Pleasures

Here are more ideas of fun things to do with your kids:

- Sit on the floor and create posters with markers, crayons and paints.

- Dance to music. Take turns being DJ.

- Play cards.

- Make greeting cards.

- Create a game.

- Get chalk and create sidewalk or driveway art.

- Gather old magazines and create collages.

Gather old magazines and create collages.

Family Matters: Reminiscing, Storytelling and Volunteering

Every family has moments they want to remember. Recalling memories, and building new ones, is another great way to spend family time.

Memorable Play

Tape record or videotape a conversation with your children about what they enjoy. What games do your children like to play now? What games did you like to play when you were a kid? What games do your kids remember playing when they were younger? Look for elements these games may have in common. This makes a wonderful multi-generational activity. Even the youngest ones can participate.

What if … You Got to Know Each Other Better

Have a brainstorming session and create a list of creative "what-if" questions. Put the questions in a box, and every so often draw one out for a fun and different mealtime topic.

Here are some examples:

- If you were a piece of fruit, what would you be and why?

- If you were a fence, what would you fence in and why?

- If you were an animal, what type would you be and why?

Mealtime topic: If you were an animal, what kind would you be?

Create a Holiday

Make up a day to celebrate something that has significance for just you and your family – make a tribute, go on a picnic, or write a silly verse. Some possible "occasions" could be:

- The first day of summer

  - Swimming lesson graduation day

    - The day our ancestors immigrated

      - The day grandpa met grandma

Write Away

Find a pen pal or e-mail pal. Children love mail, and writing is a great way to get relatives to know each other and keep in touch. Reach out to aunts, uncles and grandparents. Make it even more special by creating a pen pal title – Director of Family Correspondence.

Parent's Day Out

Give each child a turn to have undivided time with mom or dad for a whole day. Pick activities the child likes and have an established budget. Maybe the day centers around a movie or some other special activity … how sweet it is to have a whole day with no competition for a parent's attention!

Be Board

Take an afternoon or evening to play some of your kid's favorite board games. If you have more than one child, let them take turns choosing which game to play.

Field Trips – Far and Wide

It's fun to explore and learn together. As you plan your family field trips, try to give yourself new experiences by visiting places you've never been or doing things you've never done. For the greatest educational impact, tell your children stories about the places you are visiting and ask them to write about the trip afterwards. You can even create a scrapbook of your adventure.

Look for the History

Look for local areas of historic interest, read about them, then experience them first hand. If part of the Lewis and Clark or Oregon Trail is near your home, read up on the explorers and their adventures, then walk or camp near the trail. This makes history come to life. Talk about what's different today. Imagine how you would feel if you were those courageous explorers.

For a real "taste" of history, research what kinds of food they might have eaten and make a similar version.

For a real "taste" of history, research what kinds of food they might have eaten and make a similar version.

Visit your Farmer's Market.

To Market

During the late spring and early summer, make a Saturday morning trip to your Farmer's Market. In many cities, farmers from all over the area bring in fresh produce and baked goods. Often there's music and entertainment. People are friendly and interested in talking about what they grow and how they grow it.

This is a good time to learn about different kinds of fruits and vegetables, to pick up gardening tips, to buy produce and to have a leisurely outdoor family morning.

Farm Bred

Contact local farms in your area and see if they're open to visitors. Springtime can be a magical time to see baby chicks, lambs and calves. Plus, you get to learn a little about the hard work of farming.

Free Floating

Plan your vacations ahead. See which days museums and other attractions offer free admission and arrange your visit to take advantage of these days. It's a great way to see a lot and spend little.

Choose A Field Trip

Have multi-family field trips. Take turns letting one family host and plan each trip. Think of fascinating factories, museums or other places you'd like to go. Some examples include: the courthouse, food manufacturers, wastewater treatment plants, farms, manufacturing plants and sports facilities. Come up with some questions to talk about before the trip. Invite each child to write or draw a story of the trip and include these in a thank you note you send to the person who gave the tour.

The Best of the Best

Speaking of being connoisseurs ... pick a favorite family activity, such as miniature golf or eating barbecue. Make it a family project to visit every location that fits the category and rate it on a special family score card to select "the best in town." Let everyone add a category to the list.

Action, Camera

Home movies can provide an endless source of entertainment options ... both watching and making them. Take videos of simple daily stuff, like baking together or going to the park together. Plan a play, a concert, do your own version of a book, movie or music video as a family. Let the kids direct and then pop some popcorn. Sit with them as they watch their creation.

Helping Hands

Find volunteer work your family can do together. Some families work in soup kitchens, and some volunteer in centers for families with sick children. Others visit shut-ins. One family tape-recorded a special collection of stories for a children's hospital.

Contact volunteer agencies, such as United Way, to find out what kinds of family-oriented volunteer projects they recommend.

Do something that lets your children connect with people who live differently than they do. Here are some ideas:

- Create a book on tape for an ailing friend or relative or a children's hospital

- Create a cartoon scrapbook for a hospital or sick friend

- Serve at a soup kitchen

Home movies can provide an endless source of entertainment.

- Read to shut-ins
- Visit nursing homes and elders
- Work in a garden
- Do simple home repairs
- Stuff envelopes
- Staff a thrift shop
- Help in a charity-based holiday store
- Bake cookies to sell at a fundraising event

Take your family bowling at a time when the prices are inexpensive.

Good Old-Fashioned Fun

Here are a few more ideas that are relatively inexpensive and provide everyone some fun.

- Take your family bowling at a time when the prices are inexpensive.

- Go to the batting cages. Everyone can take a turn.

- Visit the discounted movie theaters. Save money by bringing your own snacks (provided the theater will let you).

- Walk or ride bikes to the ice cream shop and share an ice cream treat.

Taking time to do some of these activities will deepen your relationship with your children and will also make your life more fun.

Dear Reader:

Do you have an idea you'd like to have included in a future edition of *Yes, You Can ... Afford to Raise A Family*? If so, please contact:

Alexis Preston
Editor
Stowers Innovations, Inc.
4500 Main
Kansas City, MO 64111
E-mail: info@stowers-innovations.com

GLOSSARY:

Words and terms used throughout this book have been defined here with simple explanations. More detailed definitions may be found in financial dictionaries, as well as in the books and Web sites listed under "Additional Resources" in this book.

account – term used to describe money held by a bank or an investment company for the depositor.

allowance – a planned sum of money (either given on a regular basis or for chores done) that helps children learn money management.

annual report – a yearly record of an organization's financial condition distributed to shareholders. Included in the report is a description of the organization's operations, balance sheet and income statement.

appreciation – an increase in the value of an asset (such as a stock, bond, mutual fund or real estate) over time.

asset – anything that can be sold or has an exchange value. This includes savings, property, stocks and collectibles.

ATM (Automated Teller Machine) – a machine at which people can perform banking transactions, such as withdrawing, transferring or depositing money from their accounts.

barter – to trade articles and services without using money.

bond – a security that obligates the issuer to pay the bondholder a specified sum of money, usually at specific intervals, and to repay the principal amount of the loan at maturity. Bondholders have an IOU from the issuer, but no corporate ownership privileges, as stockholders do.

budget – a financial plan in which income and expenses are estimated and compared for a specified time period.

capital gains – the positive difference between the purchase price and the selling price of an asset; a profit from the sale of investments or property.

certificate of deposit (CD) – a type of federally-insured savings account in which a depositor agrees to lend their money to a bank for a predetermined amount of time. Cash withdrawn prior to the maturity date may incur a substantial penalty.

check – a written order to a financial institution to pay a specified amount of money to a particular person or company from money in the depositor's account.

checkbook balancing – the act of comparing the numbers in your checkbook against those on your bank statement to make certain neither you or the bank has made an error.

common stock – units or shares of a public corporation which are available to be purchased by the public. Purchasing shares of common stock is considered an owner investment.

compounding – when your money earns interest, not only on the principal, but also on any interest that was earned earlier. For example, if you have $100 growing at 10% per year, it will be $110 in one year (having increased by $10), and then $121 in the second year (having increased by $11), and $133 in the third year (having increased by $12).

consumer – a person who trades their money for goods and services.

coupons – certificates offering discounts on goods or services.

credit card – a plastic card issued by a bank, retail store or other creditor giving consumers the right to purchase goods or services and pay for them later. Most credit cards offer a grace period during which interest is not charged. After that, consumers are charged interest on the balance until it is paid off.

currency – any kind of money that is used as a form of exchange.

custodian – the person (usually a parent) who is responsible for a minor child's savings or investment account.

deposit – cash, checks or securities given to a bank or other institution for credit to the customer's account.

discount broker – a stockbroker who buys or sells your stock or bond orders but, unlike a "full-service broker," does not give you advice on your investments.

diversification – buying securities of different investment types, industry types, risk levels and companies in order to reduce your level of risk (or loss) if something should damage the business of any one of your investment holdings.

dividends – money a shareholder receives from a company as a result of the company earning a profit.

Dow Jones Industrial Average (the Dow) – an indicator showing generally how the stock market is going. The Dow is an average of the prices of 30 stocks which represent a wide array of industry types.

electronic transactions – financial dealings that are made through the use of computers.

expenses – the amount paid for goods and services.

Federal Deposit Insurance Corporation (FDIC) – this federal agency insures (within limits) your funds on deposit in member institutions. Banks and institutions pay the FDIC to insure individual deposits and protect their customers from possible loss.

Federal Reserve – a system of 12 regional reserve banks. Each Federal Reserve bank monitors the commercial and savings banks in its region to make certain they follow industry regulations. The reserve banks act as depositories for member banks in their regions, providing money transfers and other services.

fixed income – an investment that pays a predetermined rate of return, such as a bond, CD or savings account.

gross pay – total amount of a salary before taxes, insurance, benefits and other expenses are taken out.

income – money earned from work, investments and the sale of goods or services.

interest – the cost for the use of borrowed money paid by the borrower. For example, you receive interest when you allow a bank to use your money. You pay interest when you borrow money from a bank.

investment – using money, time or energy to create more money or reach a goal. Investments can either be financial (where money is invested to reach a financial goal) or can be an investment of time, talent and effort on the part of an individual (such as an investment in a college education to achieve future career success).

lender investment – an investment in which a bank or financial institution borrows your money in exchange for a set sum of money (interest). At the end of the loan period, the full amount you lent is returned to you. Examples of lender investments include savings accounts, CDs and money market accounts.

liability – debts or financial commitments.

liquidity – the ability to convert your assets into cash. The easier it is to get cash from an investment the more "liquid" the investment.

loan – a transaction in which an amount of money is borrowed for a specified period of time with the agreement that the money will be paid back to the lender within a certain time period. The loan often involves interest paid to the lender by the borrower.

mentor – a wise and trusted counselor or teacher.

money market – an account which invests in short-term investments (such as CDs and treasury bills) and offers checkwriting abilities. Typically, money market accounts require a minimum deposit and limit the number of checks that can be written over a given time period. Funds are available to depositors at any time without penalty.

mutual fund – a professionally managed investment portfolio that offers individuals the ability to invest in a collection of stocks or stocks and bonds put together for a specific goal, such as growth, income or capital preservation.

negotiation – the act of talking to others with the hope of gaining a more favorable deal on a purchased item.

net pay – the amount of salary received after taxes, insurance, benefits and other expenses have been taken out.

owner investment – an investment in which you become part (or full) owner of a business or property, thereby sharing in some of the risks and rewards of ownership. Examples of owner investments include mutual funds, common stocks, real estate and collectibles.

profit – a positive difference between the purchase price and selling price. If the selling price is higher than the purchase price, there is a profit.

resource – individual assets (such as money, property, other people, talent or skill) that can be used to support or help you reach a goal.

return – used to describe the money made (or lost) on an investment.

risk – the probability that an original investment might drop in value; the chance of non-payment of a debt.

savings – money that is held or collected for future use.

share – a single unit of ownership in a corporation or mutual fund.

shareholder – a person who owns stock (or shares) in a company.

stockbroker – a person who facilitates the buying and selling of securities, such as stocks or bonds. As payment for services, commission is collected based upon a percentage of the value of the transaction or assets.

NOTES

_____ _____

_____ _____

_____ _____

_____ _____

_____ _____

_____ _____

_____ _____

_____ _____

Discover the Good Life ™

Use this order form to get more practical information to help you on the road to financial freedom. Or, check your favorite bookstore to get additional copies of *Yes, You Can ... Afford to Raise a Family* or any of our other titles.

Name: _____

Address: _____

City: _____ State: _____ Zip: _____

Phone: _____

Email Address: _____

☐ Check here to receive our FREE quarterly INSIGHTS e-newsletter

Would you like to belong to our Product Survey Advisory Board and help us develop new concepts? ☐ Yes ☐ No
As a member of the board, you will get FREE advance samples of our concepts for your review and comments.

	QUANTITY @ PRICE	TOTAL
Yes, You Can ... Achieve Financial Independence	@ $19.95 each	
Yes, You Can ... Afford to Raise a Family	@ $19.95 each	
Yes, You Can ... Raise Financially Aware Kids	@ $19.95 each	
The Good Life CD-ROM	@ $9.95 each	
10 Proven Ideas to Help You Eliminate Credit Card Debt	@ FREE limit 1	FREE
10 Proven Ideas That Could Improve Your Financial Position	@ FREE limit 1	FREE
Yes, We Can ... Understand Money – Kids Activity Book	@ FREE limit 1	FREE
	Shipping and Handling	
	Sub-Total	
	Sales Tax MO residents please add sales tax	
	TOTAL	

☐ My check is enclosed.

Please make your check payable and return to:

**Stowers Innovations Inc.
c/o IFS
210 NW Plaza Drive
Kansas City, MO 64150-9806**

☐ Please charge my credit card.

☐ VISA®   ☐ MasterCard®   ☐ Discover®

☐ American Express®

Card Number: _____

Expiration Date: _____

Signature: _____

CUT HERE ✂

If you prefer, you may call us at 1-800-234-3445 or visit our Web site at www.stowers-innovations.com.

RF2004